Aaron Maree's

CLASSIC DESSERTS

Angus&Robertson

An imprint of HarperCollins*Publishers*

Angus&Robertson
An imprint of HarperCollins*Publishers*, Australia

First published in Australia in 1995

HarperCollins*Publishers*
25 Ryde Road, Pymble, Sydney NSW 2073, Australia
31 View Road, Glenfield, Auckland 10, New Zealand
Hazelton Lanes, 55 Avenue Road, Suite 2900, Toronto, Ontario M5R 3L2
and 1995 Markham Road, Scarborough, Ontario M1B 5M8, Canada
77–84 Fulham Palace Road, London W6 8JB, United Kingdom
10 East 53rd Street, New York NY 10022, USA

National Library of Australia Cataloguing-in-Publication data:

Maree, Aaron.
Aaron Maree's Classic Desserts
Includes Index.

ISBN 0 207 18026 1.
1. Desserts. I. Title. II. Title: Classic desserts.
641.86

Photographer: Andre Martin
Food stylist: Donna Hay
Cover Photograph: Blueberry Yoghurt Mousse Cups, page 50

Printed in Hong Kong
9 8 7 6 5 4 3 2 1   98 97 96 95

CONTENTS

'After eating, an epicure gives a thin smile of satisfaction;
a gastronome, burping into his napkin, praises the food in a magazine;
a gourmet, repressing his burp, criticises the food in the same magazine;
a gourmand belches happily and tells everybody where he ate.'

William Safire, New York Times, January 1985

Dedication

This book is dedicated to my family, who have supported me through all my endeavours,
great and small, over the past few years.
To my parents especially I say thanks — I hope that one day I will actually
find time to cook for them!

Acknowledgments

The author would like to thank the following people for their assistance in the development
of recipes, for personal assistance, or just for their support as friends.
Michael Pridmore and John Reid, *Defiance Flour Mills*
Bill Starr, *Breville and Kenwood Kitchen Appliances*
John Dart, *Trumps Nuts and Dried Fruits*
Joanne Hardy
Racheal Creek, Rod Slater and Trish Fields, *Cadbury Confectionery*
Paul Frizell and Darryl Jackson, *Australian Quality Egg Farms*
Jan Liddle, *Glad Products of Australia*
Robert Hill Smith, Peter Sawrey and S. Smith and Sons, of the wine labels *Yalumba*,
Heggies, Eden Valley and *Pewsay Vale*
Frank Hese, *CSR Sugar*
Alan Plumb, *Chef's Pride* and *Creative Gourmet* products
Bernadette Roach, *McCormicks Foods*
Mr M. Choo, *Bonlac Foods* and *Western Star Butter* products

Orrefors Kosta Boda: Miranda, Mosman and David Jones stores
Ventura Design
Villeroy & Boch

Introduction

The greatest inspiration for my writing has always been the desire to provide books that had all the things in them that I could never find in books when I was studying. I never thought that I would have the chance to write so many books on the subject I love, and be able to dissect that subject into its most important areas — cakes, cookies, confectionery, chocolate and now some of the most well-known dessert classics of all times.

What makes this book different (I hope) from most books on classic dishes is that I have personally selected, during my first decade of pastrycooking, my favourite dishes from around the world. Dishes that I have cooked on my travels, in some cases, and in other cases, dishes that I have simply eaten, enjoyed, and wish now to share with others interested in finding the best recipes for classic desserts.

Every year I travel the world, for work, pleasure, competitions, or merely for recipe hunting. I always seem to end up in the kitchen after a really good meal, talking with the chef about the dishes I have just enjoyed or, in some tough cases, discussing the extensive menu from which I have found it too difficult to select a dessert. Sometimes, I have had to venture into the pastry kitchen to look at all the desserts, request a sample of the lot and then leave the final choice to my palate.

I have long felt that whilst we must never lose touch with our true classic recipes and their original methods of production, modern innovative cooking allows us to create our own interpretations of these recipes. In this book some recipes are in their original classic form, while others are in the style in which they have been served to me or by me. I have presented them in the way I feel personally happy with. Every one has had to pass the pleasure test of my palate.

In my previous books readers have seen some of my personal interpretations of classic cake, cookie (biscuit) and confectionery recipes and have either liked, loved or been sceptical of the results. This book is my interpretation of the classic desserts in four further areas of the dessert kitchen: ice creams, mousses, puddings and afternoon tea pastries.

Whilst many of the classic recipes started with the formulation of ingredients into mixtures by renowned chefs and culinary experts, there are some recipes which have evolved slowly over centuries, having first developed from the simplest ideas and using the basic tools available at the time. Such recipes include flatbreads and pancakes, first cooked on open flat rocks in crude batter forms made from water and grains, or specialties such as the German Baumkuchen, which began life as a batter poured over a rotating stick.

Ice Creams and Sorbets

Today ice cream is a popular food found in almost every country in the world, and it makes up a large portion of the snack food market. This aside, it is still gratifying to actually produce one's own ice creams and sorbets.

Ice creams and sorbets began their culinary evolution before the birth of Christ, as a flavoured ice, possible from an accidental pouring or dropping of honey onto snow, possibly with the addition of herbs and spices. The recipe did not change much for many centuries — the only changes were more elaborate additions to the ice (flowers, fruits and juices) as people's taste buds became more demanding. Eventually, with the addition of milk or cream by an enterprising gourmet, began the quest for a more creamier ice.

Marco Polo brought a recipe for a snow-based dessert which used goat's milk, fruit, honey and ic, from China to Italy. The Italians eventually replaced the milk with cream and later, with the invention of churning, they added buttermilk and whipped cream, and before long the snow-based recipe was replaced by a purely milk-based recipe; a crude form of *crème anglaise*.

In the early 1500s, Bernardo Buontalenti discovered the freezing effects of salt and ice, and when Catherine de Medici moved to France in 1533 to marry King Henry II of France, her court chef took the recipe for his iced creams with him. Eventually the recipes and the love of ice cream spread to the newly opened coffee houses, frequented by the wealthy. Ice cream was still only available during winter, though, as a way to store iced goods had still not been found.

Several centuries later, with the invention of better *sorbetières* and of freezing facilities, ice creams went into mass production, with the first factory being opened in Baltimore, USA, during the mid to late 1800s.

The favourite ice cream recipes in this book can be produced with or without an ice cream machine. Remember, too, that instructions will change for the freezing process from machine to machine. If you do not have an ice cream machine, simply remove the mixture from your freezer every 1 to 2 hours and beat it by hand (or mix it quickly in a food processor) for 3 to 4 minutes before refreezing. Of course the type of freezing and churning process will affect the finished product: lightness, aeration, how hard it will set, and how icy it will become can all vary.

Another cause of differences in the recipes will of course be the tired old problem for food authors of differences in products between countries. High water content in milks or creams, varying acid contents of fruits, alcohol strengths and many other differences can play a large part in the success or failure of recipes and these should be considered when using all recipes.

Mousses

This chapter is also for those who prefer the lighter style of desserts. This section is high on my favourites list because most of the recipes are easy and relatively fuss-free to produce, and they vary enormously: they can be heavy or light, rich or subtle in flavour. In this section there is really a recipe for every occasion and every season.

Before you work with recipes from this chapter, though, it helps if you have a clear understanding of the differences between recipes, and know the basic definitions of mousse, fool and whips. Mousses are generally lightened by both cream and egg whites, and can be based on fruit, chocolate or other flavours. Traditionally, mousses were unset, adding to their lightness, but it has become acceptable to use a small amount of gelatine to help set a mousse. A good chocolate mousse, though, should still contain no gelatine — use the chocolate content as the setting agent.

Fools and whips only contain gelatine for presentation purposes. A fool uses only whipped cream for its body, but a whip should use only egg white. Some recipes in both classes now contain both, though.

The true beauty of these recipes is the fact that flavours can be changed easily, with the substituting of fruit pastes and purées, and the changing of dark chocolate to milk or white, usually with little or no change to the rest of the recipe.

Puddings

The puddings section includes many of the most famed recipes. The influence of my time working in England is clearly evident in this section — England is the home of many of the world's great puddings, and every borough of that country serves its puddings in its own manner.

Included in this section are the egg-based delights such as Diplomat Pudding, Queen of Puddings, Brioche and Butter Pudding and the French batter pudding Clafoutis.

Fruit plays an important role in this chapter as well, with the inclusion of Lemon Possit, a rich velvety cream, as well as Rhubarb Crumble, Apple Fritters and Baked Apples, and the summer sensation of Muscat Pears.

Not to be forgotten, though, are the comfort food puddings which make winter such a memorable season — Chocolate Pudding with a Melting Middle, Steamed Sponge Pudding, College Pudding and a favourite over the past decade, Sticky Toffee and Date Pudding.

Pastries

The recipes in the final chapter in this collection of classics are selected from my years of making sweet delicacies for the afternoon tea trolleys in several parts of the world. The English require the traditional fruit cake, jalousie and Swiss rolls, while the European afternoon tea would not be the same without Lemon Curd Tartlets, Strudel and light mousse-based treats such as Strawberry Delice. In Australia the true High Tea begins with scones, jam and cream, while a quick afternoon tea on the run in the USA would never have been the same if I had not served chocolate-covered doughnuts.

This is truly a chapter with a recipe for everybody and every taste bud!

Whether you cook these favourite classic desserts and treats, or are simply served them by another cook or chef, remember to enjoy and indulge!

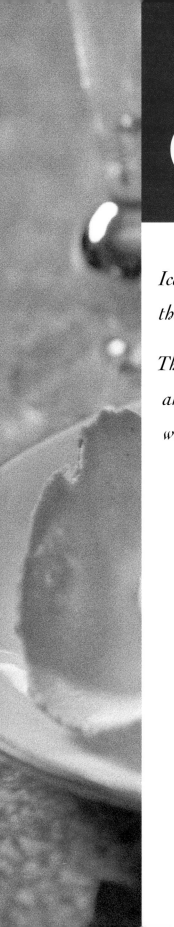

ICE CREAMS

Ice creams are popular throughout the world, especially as snack food.

These recipes are simple to prepare, and will tantalise your taste buds with a mixture of traditional and exotic flavours.

Vanilla Ice Cream

This traditional favourite can be used as the base for many variations and is used in many desserts. From this recipe you can produce virtually any flavour imaginable.

4 cups (1 litre/32 fl oz) milk

1 vanilla pod

6 egg yolks

1½ cups (375 g/12 oz) sugar

2 cups (500 ml/16 fl oz) double (whipping) cream, lightly whipped

Place the milk and the vanilla pod in a saucepan and bring to the boil.

In a large bowl, whisk the egg yolks and sugar until light and creamy. Pour the hot milk into the egg yolk mixture, whisking continuously.

Return the mixture to the saucepan and stir it over gentle heat until the mixture coats the back of the spoon. Remove the mixture from the heat and let it cool. Take out the vanilla pod, split it and scrape its seeds back into the mixture.

Fold through the cream, then pour the mixture into an ice cream machine, or into a bowl. Place the bowl in the freezer.

If the mixture is in the freezer, stir it rapidly every hour for 2 to 3 minutes. Continue this procedure until the mixture is of ice cream consistency. If it is in an ice cream machine, churn until the mixture freezes.

Serve when firm enough to scoop.

Variations

Orange and Chocolate Chip

Add the zest of 2 oranges, cut into fine strips, and 90 g (3 oz) of chocolate chips.

Coffee

Add ½ cup (90 g /3 oz) of crushed espresso coffee beans.

Cookies and Cream

Break 1 cup (125 g/4 oz) of chocolate cream-filled biscuits (such as Oreos) into small pieces and fold these through the ice cream.

Berry

Fold through ½ cup (90 g/3 oz) of berry purée. Alternatively, freeze the berries on a tray, to prevent them becoming mushy, then fold them gently through the ice cream.

Triple Chocolate

Chop 45 g (1½ oz) each of white, milk and dark chocolate into small pieces and fold these through the ice cream.

Nuts

Chop ½ cup (60 g/2 oz) of your favourite nuts into pieces and roast them for 12 to 15 minutes on a baking tray in the oven, to bring out their flavour. When they are cool, fold them through the ice cream.

Previous page: A selection of ice creams and sorbets served in Tuile Cups, page 120

Spiced Chocolate Ice Cream

A rich and satisfying frozen delight made from cream and condensed milk rather than from the usual crème anglaise base. If recipes came any easier than this, you wouldn't need a cookbook — they would just appear, finished !

This ice cream is for those who do not have an ice cream churn.

In a bowl, lightly whip the cream until it forms soft peaks.

Mix the condensed milk and the chocolate, then fold this through the cream. Fold through the spices, then pour the mixture into a bowl and freeze for 2 to 3 hours before serving.

2½ cups (625 ml/20 fl oz) double (whipping) cream

1 cup (250 ml/8 fl oz) sweetened condensed milk

155 g (5 oz) dark (plain or semi-sweet) chocolate, melted

¼ teaspoon cinnamon

¼ teaspoon ground cloves

¼ teaspoon Chinese five spice or garam masala

Crunchy Coffee Ice Cream

6 tablespoons water

¾ cup (185 g/6 oz) sugar

8 egg yolks

⅓ cup (90 g/3 oz) sugar

3 tablespoons instant coffee granules

½ cup (125 ml/4 fl oz) brandy

3 tablespoons crushed espresso coffee beans

2⅓ cups (560 ml/18 fl oz) double (whipping) cream, lightly whipped

Place the water and sugar in a saucepan and bring to the boil. Boil for 1 to 2 minutes, but do not allow the syrup to caramelise.

In a bowl, whisk the egg yolks and sugar until light and fluffy, and creamy in colour.

Slowly drizzle the syrup into the egg yolk mixture. Continue whisking until all the syrup is incorporated and the mixture cools.

Dissolve the coffee granules in the brandy and fold this and the crushed coffee beans into the mixture. Fold through the cream.

Pour the mixture into a dish and freeze it, or place it in an ice cream machine and churn until the mixture freezes.

Serve with crystallised orange zest.

Frozen Chocolate Decadence

Little needs to be said of this dish — I now work almost exclusively in chocolate and this is a creation par excellence.

If you are a chocoholic, this will probably remain on your must-cook list for as long as you live!

Place ½ cup (125 ml/4 fl oz) of cream in a saucepan and bring to the boil. Remove from the heat, add the melted chocolate and stir until a thick paste is formed. Let this mixture cool.

In a bowl, whisk the egg yolks, sugar and finely grated orange zest until light and creamy.

Place the milk in a saucepan and bring to the boil. Whisk the boiled milk into the egg yolk mixture. Continue whisking until ingredients are combined. Let this mixture cool.

Fold the chocolate mixture into the milk and egg yolk mixture. When this is cool, fold in the lightly whipped cream and the liqueur.

Freeze overnight, then serve small scoops in Tuile Cups (see page 120).

½ cup (125 ml/4 fl oz) double (whipping) cream

310 g (10 oz) dark (plain or semi-sweet) chocolate, melted

5 egg yolks

⅓ cup (90 g/3 oz) sugar

finely grated zest of 1 orange

1 cup (250 ml/8 fl oz) milk

1½ cups (375 ml/12 fl oz) double (whipping) cream, lightly whipped

2 tablespoons Drambuie

White Chocolate and Coffee Ice Cream

A fantastic combination of white chocolate and coffee which makes for a sweet, aromatic and delightful dessert, delicious served on its own or served with chocolate desserts.

1 cup (185 g/6 oz) sultanas (golden raisins)

½ cup (125 ml/4 fl oz) brandy

2½ cups (625 ml/20 fl oz) double (whipping) cream

1 cup (250 ml/8 fl oz) sweetened condensed milk

225 g (7 oz) white chocolate, melted

1½ tablespoons instant coffee granules or powder

1 tablespoon hot water

Soak the sultanas in the brandy for 1 to 2 days before making the ice cream.

In a bowl, whip the cream until it forms soft peaks. Warm the condensed milk in a saucepan over a gentle heat, then quickly fold through the melted white chocolate.

Dissolve the coffee granules in the hot water, then add this to the cream mixture.

Fold through the brandy-soaked sultanas, then pour the mixture into a 7 x 25 x 7 cm (3 x 12 x 3 in) log-shaped container or loaf tin.

Freeze overnight and serve thin slices on a Chocolate Sauce (see page 114) or with fresh Raspberry Sauce (see page 53).

Frozen Chocolate Decadence

Caramelised Brown Bread Ice Cream

14 slices brown (wholemeal) bread

1½ cups (375 g/12 oz) demerara sugar

7 egg yolks

⅔ cup (155 g/5 oz) sugar

2 cups (500 ml/16 fl oz) single (light) cream

This is a light, but very rich, dessert that will be the talking point of any meal. The trick to it is to be careful when you caramelise the brown bread — it tends to burn easily. Serve with a rich Chocolate Sauce (see page 114) to really delight.

This ice cream is chunky, and cannot be made using an ice cream machine or churn.

Cut the crusts from the bread. Place the slices on a tray and sprinkle them with the demerara sugar. Place the sugared bread under a grill until the sugar caramelises. Move the bread mixture occasionally, to ensure all sugar is caramelised. Remove the bread and let it cool, then break it into small pieces.

In a large bowl, whisk the egg yolks and sugar until they form a thick sabayon (are pale, light, and fluffy).

In another bowl, whip the cream until it forms soft peaks.

Fold the cream through the egg yolk mixture, then fold in the caramelised brown bread. Pour the mixture into a large container — a 7 x 25 x 7 cm (3 x 12 x 3 in) loaf tin — or terrine moulds or a 20 cm (8 in) springform cake tin, and freeze it overnight.

Serve in slices with Chocolate Sauce (see page 114).

Cinnamon and Black Pepper Parfait

This magnificent combination of flavours is an unusual mixture of gentle coolness and hot spiciness. Use fresh cracked black pepper for the full flavour of this delicious dessert to come through.

3 egg yolks

⅔ cup (125 g/4 oz) icing (powdered) sugar

1½ cups (375 ml/12 fl oz) single (light) cream, lightly whipped

2 egg whites

2 tablespoons sugar

2 teaspoons ground cinnamon

2 teaspoons cracked black pepper

Whisk the egg yolks and the icing sugar in a large bowl over a bain-marie (or double saucepan) until the mixture reaches the thick and creamy sabayon (ribbon) stage. Fold the cream through.

Whisk the egg whites until they form soft peaks, then slowly add the sugar. Continue whisking until all the sugar is dissolved.

Fold the egg white mixture through the egg yolk/cream mixture, then add the cinnamon and black pepper. Pour the mixture into a log-shaped mould or loaf tin 7 x 20 x 7 cm (3 x 8 x 3 in). Cover and freeze for 6 hours, or overnight.

Cut into slices and serve immediately with Langue de Chat Biscuits (see page 119), or with warm Cherry Compote (see page 113).

Mascarpone Ice Cream

Place the milk, cream and sugar in a saucepan and bring slowly to the boil.

Let the mixture cool slightly, then add the egg yolks, one at a time, beating well after each addition.

Place the mascarpone in a bowl. Slowly add the milk and cream mixture, stirring until the mixture forms a smooth paste.

Place the mixture (in the bowl) in the freezer or in an ice cream machine.

If your mixture is in the freezer, stir it every half hour for several minutes, then refreeze. Repeat this procedure until the mixture is completely frozen and takes on the consistency of ice cream. If you are using an ice cream machine, churn until the mixture freezes.

4 cups (1 litre/32 fl oz) milk

1 cup (250 ml/8 fl oz) double (whipping) cream

1½ cups (310 g/10 oz) sugar

5 egg yolks

375 g (12 oz) mascarpone

Jerusalem Artichoke Ice Cream

250 g (250 g/8 oz) Jerusalem artichoke

1½ cups (375 ml/12 fl oz) milk

8 egg yolks

¼ cup (90 ml/3 fl oz) liquid glucose (corn syrup)

2 tablespoons Grand Marnier

½ cup (125 ml/4 fl oz) double (whipping) cream

Orange Caramel Sauce

⅓ cup (90 ml/3 fl oz) water

1 cup (250 g/8 oz) sugar

6 teaspoons unsalted butter

finely grated zest of 4 oranges

1 tablespoon Grand Marnier

This unusual ice cream has a rough texture but a divine flavour, and is best served simply, in a Tuile Cup (see page 120) or in a dark (plain or semi-sweet) Chocolate Basket (see page 122).

Wash the artichokes, then boil them in ½ cup (125 ml/4 fl oz) of milk in a small saucepan. When they are cooked, drain and mash them. In a bowl, lightly whisk the egg yolks and glucose. Boil the remainder of the milk. Add the milk to the mashed artichokes and the Grand Marnier, then mix in the egg yolks and glucose. Fold through the lightly whipped cream.

Pour the mixture into a mould or tin and freeze overnight. If an ice cream machine is being used, churn until frozen, then mould the ice cream.

Serve with Orange Caramel Sauce.

Orange Caramel Sauce

Place the water and sugar in a saucepan and bring to the boil. Continue boiling until the mixture is a pale amber colour.

Remove the mixture from the heat and stir in the butter. Then add the orange zest and Grand Marnier. Serve the sauce warm.

Gelato

Gelato is the Italian version of the French sorbet. It is virtually the same, but a good gelato should always be slightly icier than its French counterpart.

¾ cup (185 g/6 oz) sugar

½ cup (125 ml/4 fl oz) orange juice

juice and finely grated zest of 1 lemon

2 cups (500 ml/16 fl oz) water

3 egg whites

½ cup (90 g/3 oz) icing (powdered) sugar, extra

Place the sugar, orange juice, lemon zest and juice and water in a large saucepan and bring slowly to the boil. Boil the mixture, uncovered, for 8 minutes. Let it cool. When the mixture is cold, pour it into a large tray and freeze it for 24 hours.

In a large bowl, whisk the egg whites and the icing sugar until they form stiff peaks. Remove the frozen ice, break it up into fine pieces and add it to the egg whites. Whisk until thoroughly combined.

Pour the mixture back into the tray and freeze it for 24 hours before serving.

Berry Sorbet

This tart and refreshing sorbet can be made from one kind of berry only, or from a medley of berries for a 'berry, berry' nice dessert.

¾ cup (185 ml/6 fl oz) water

1 cup (250 g/8 oz) sugar

310 g (10 oz) frozen berries — strawberries, raspberries, blackberries, etc.

juice and finely grated zest of 2 lemons

Place the water and sugar in a saucepan and bring to the boil. Boil the syrup for 3 minutes.

Purée the berries, then strain them, to remove any seeds. Add the purée to the syrup.

Add the lemon juice and zest. Let the mixture cool.

Freeze the mixture in an ice cream machine or in the freezer. If the mixture is in the freezer, remove it after 2 to 3 hours and stir well (or mix in a food processor) for 2 to 3 minutes. Refreeze, then repeat twice more. If it is in an ice cream machine, churn until the mixture freezes.

Serve on its own, or with fresh fruit.

Berry Sorbet and Gelato

Mango Sorbet

flesh of 2 ripe mangoes

juice and zest of 1 orange

2 egg whites

¼ cup (60 g/2 oz) sugar

During summer, one of my favourite flavours is the sweet seductive taste of fresh mango. Mango in puddings, sauces and this delicious sorbet is an absolute joy.

Use the freshest of mangoes to ensure a magnificent flavour to this sorbet. It is heaven, either on its own or served with other light desserts. (If fresh mango is simply unavailable, use canned mango flesh.)

Purée the flesh of the mango, then mix it with the orange juice and zest. Place this mixture in a flat container such as a jelly roll pan, and freeze it until it begins to firm.

In a large bowl, whisk the egg whites until they form stiff peaks. Slowly add the sugar. Keep whisking the egg whites until all the sugar is dissolved.

Remove the freezing mango flesh and stir it till smooth. Fold the mango mixture into the egg whites. Pour the mixture into a container and freeze for 4 to 5 hours, or overnight.

Mandarin and Rockmelon Ice

This is a fine combination of fruits which are often neglected on the dessert menu. Oranges can be used instead of mandarins, but the delicate balance of fruit flavours really does rely on the mandarin, which has a softer and more aromatic flavour than the orange.

2½ cups (625 ml/20 fl oz) water

1½ cups (375 g/12 oz) sugar

405 g (13 oz) can of mandarin segments

225 g (7 oz) rockmelon flesh, cleaned

¼ cup (60 ml/2 fl oz) lemon juice

2 tablespoons Grand Marnier or other orange liqueur

Place the water and sugar in a saucepan and bring slowly to the boil, then boil for 3 to 4 minutes.

This dish is a favourite with summer puddings and desserts or on its own during spring and for light summer meals.

Purée the mandarin segments and the rockmelon together, then strain the mixture through a sieve into a large bowl. Add the lemon juice and liqueur, then the syrup, and combine well.

Pour the liquid into a tray and let it cool. When it is cool, place the tray in the freezer and freeze the mixture overnight.

Using a whisk or a fork, break up the mixture into pieces and mix slightly. Refreeze for 1 hour, then serve with fresh fruit.

Claret Ice

One of the simplest ways of creating a divine dessert is to freeze the wine one would normally drink with the meal. This easy ice recipe is quite sweet, and can be served as part of another dessert, or to accompany cake or fruits. It is also great for those who have eaten too much but still want a light, refreshing, sweet end to the meal.

You can substitute white wine for the red wine, but it is the colour of the red wine that makes this such a striking accompaniment or dessert.

⅓ cup (90 ml/3 fl oz) water

1⅓ cups (340 g/11 oz) sugar

3 cups (750 ml/24 fl oz) red wine (claret)

juice and zest of 2 lemons

juice and zest of 2 oranges

Place the water and sugar in a saucepan and bring to the boil. Boil for 2 minutes. Pour the red wine into the syrup and whisk in the juice and zest of the lemon and orange. Pour the mixture into a baking tray and freeze. Break up the ice with a fork every time it becomes firm, to keep the ice crystals small.

When frozen, break the ice into small pieces and serve in champagne glasses frosted on the rim with sugar. Serve by itself in champagne glasses, or beside a rich chocolate dessert, or with fresh fruit.

Semifreddo

6 egg yolks

⅔ cup (155 g/5 oz) sugar

¾ cup (185 ml/6 fl oz) port

¼ cup (60 ml/2 fl oz) orange juice

1½ cups (375 ml/12 fl oz) double (whipping) cream, lightly whipped

90 g (3 oz) roasted flaked almonds

Semifreddo means 'semi-frozen' or 'semi-cold'. This iced dessert contains such a great quantity of sugar that it does not freeze solidly, and therefore seems not to be as cold as most iced desserts.

In a large bowl, whisk the egg yolks and sugar until light, fluffy and creamy in colour. Add the port and orange juice and combine well.

Place the bowl over a pot of simmering water and whisk until the mixture reaches the sabayon (ribbon) stage (holds the figure eight when drizzled over itself). Remove the bowl from the heat and place it over a basin of either cold water or ice. Continue whisking until the mixture is cool.

Fold through the lightly whipped cream and roasted flaked almonds, then pour the mixture into a 7 x 20 x 7 cm (3 x 8 x 3 in) loaf tin and freeze it overnight.

Serve in slices, on a Coffee Sauce (see page 114) or with a plain Vanilla Anglaise (see page 117).

Iced Orange Soufflé

Place the sugar and water in a saucepan and bring slowly to the boil. Boil to 116°C (235°F) measuring with a sugar thermometer. Add the orange zest and remove the mixture from the heat.

Place the egg yolks in the bowl of an electric mixer and begin whisking them. Slowly drizzle the hot molten sugar into the whisking egg yolks. Continue whisking until the mixture is cold.

Whip the cream until it forms soft peaks.

Add the orange juice to the cold egg yolk mixture, then fold the whipped cream through.

Pour the mixture into 4 to 6 soufflé dishes, each of which has a paper collar around the sides. Fill the dishes to 3 cm (1¼ in) higher than the actual dish. Freeze the soufflés for 4 to 5 hours, or overnight.

To serve, place fresh orange zest on top of the soufflés, remove the paper collars, and dust with icing sugar.

1 cup (250 g/8 oz) sugar

½ cup (125 ml/4 fl oz) water

finely grated zest of 2 oranges

8 egg yolks

½ cup (125 ml/4 fl oz) orange juice

2 tablespoons Drambuie

2½ cups (625 ml/20 fl oz) double (whipping) cream

icing (powdered) sugar, for serving

Paper Collars

Cut pieces of paper that are 5 cm (2 in) taller than the soufflé dishes and that have at least a 2 to 3 cm (1 in) overlap when wrapped around the dishes. Take pieces of string long enough to wrap around the dishes 3 times. Wrap the paper around the dishes, then wrap the string around twice, tightly, and tie it with a firm knot. When serving, cut the string and remove the collars.

Iced Orange Soufflé

Bombe Cecilia

500 g (16 oz) chocolate ice cream
(see page 12 or page 15)

1⅓ cups (340 g/11 oz) sugar

½ cup (125 ml/4 fl oz) water

5 egg whites

5 egg yolks

1¼ cups (310 ml/10 fl oz) single
(light) cream, lightly whipped

1¼ cups (155 g/5 oz)
roasted chopped hazelnuts

90 g (3 oz) glacé
(candied) pineapple

½ génoise sponge (see page 119)

*There are many different bombes — some are covered in meringue
(the traditional Bombe Alaska, for instance), others are decorated
elaborately on the outside. All are visually exciting when they are cut,
and you see the inside and the outside together.*

*This is my favourite bombe recipe of all. It was taught to me during my
apprenticeship by my German Master.*

Line a large (2 litre) pudding basin or soufflé ramekin (or individual ramekins)
thinly with the chocolate ice cream. Freeze until the ice cream is set firm.

Place 1 cup (250 g/8 oz) of sugar and the water in a saucepan and boil to
110°C (220°F).

In a bowl, whisk the egg whites with the remaining sugar (⅓ cup/90 g/3 oz)
until they form stiff peaks. Still whisking, drizzle the boiled sugar slowly into the
egg whites. Continue whisking until the whites are cool, then carefully whisk in
the egg yolks.

Fold the cream, hazeluts and pineapple into the mixture.

Pour the mixture into the centre of the chocolate lined mould/s and place a
thin layer of sponge on the top (when unmoulded, this will become the base).

Freeze the bombe for 6 to 8 hours, or overnight, before unmoulding,
decorating and serving.

Peach Parfait

This is a light, airy treat. Cut it into slices and serve it on a berry purée or rich sauce to round out your dining experience beautifully.

The beauty of this recipe is that any fruit can be substituted for the peach.

Purée the poached peach flesh and add the cinnamon.

In a bowl, whisk the egg yolks and sugar until light and fluffy.

In another bowl, whip the cream until soft peaks form, then fold it into the egg yolk mixture. Combine well.

In a third bowl, whisk the egg whites until soft peaks form, then slowly add the extra sugar.

Fold the egg whites through the egg yolk/cream mixture, then fold in the peach purée.

Pour the mixture into a 23 cm (9 in) springform cake tin lined with plastic wrap (cling film), and freeze overnight.

Cut the parfait into 12 slices and serve with Caramel Sauce (see page 114).

6 egg yolks

¾ cup (185 g/6 oz) sugar

flesh of 3 ripe peaches, poached lightly and peeled

1 teaspoon cinnamon

3 cups (750 ml/24 fl oz) single (light) cream

3 egg whites

2 tablespoons sugar, extra

Summer Iced Sabayon

8 egg yolks

¾ cup (185 g/6 oz) sugar

finely grated zest of 2 oranges

7 tablespoons Grand Marnier or Cointreau, or other orange liqueur

1 cup (250 ml/8 fl oz) fresh unsweetened orange juice

Place the egg yolks, sugar, orange zest and orange liqueur in a large bowl. Over a bain-marie (double saucepan) on low heat, whisk the mixture until it becomes thick and frothy. Whisk in the orange juice.

Pour the mixture into a saucepan and stir with a wooden spoon over gentle heat until the mixture coats the back of the spoon. (Do not allow the mixture to boil or simmer).

Pour the mixture into one large soufflé ramekin or 6 to 8 small ramekins, and freeze the ramekin/s overnight.

Decorate the top of each serving with a rosette of fresh cream and a piece of crystallised orange peel.

Coupe Belle Hélène

*This dessert was invented by Auguste Escoffier, to celebrate the opera
La Belle Hélène (music by Offenbach, libretto by Meilhac and Halèvy, first produced
in Paris in December, 1864). It consists of vanilla ice cream, a poached pear
and a sauce of rich chocolate.*

*I love this simple but exquisite dessert because it reminds me that Escoffier, too,
realised that pears had a greatness in desserts which had rarely been exploited.*

Place the water, lemon juice, sugar, cinnamon and cloves in a large saucepan
and bring to a gentle simmer.

Peel the pears, leaving the stalks intact, and place them in the simmering
liquid. Rest a smaller-sized lid directly on the pears to keep them submerged
and prevent them floating. Cook them until they are tender but not pulpy; until
a knife can be easily inserted into their flesh. Remove the cooked pears with a
slotted spoon and leave them to cool.

When they are cool, use a melon baller to carefully remove their cores,
starting at the base and working only three-quarters of the way to the top, so
that the stalk remains. Set the pears aside.

Chocolate Sauce

Place the cream in a saucepan and bring to the boil. Add the chopped chocolate
and allow to sit, off the heat, for 2 to 3 minutes before stirring into a smooth
sauce. Add the Poire William brandy to the cool chocolate sauce and serve.

To Assemble

Place a scoop of ice cream in the centre of an egg ring. Flatten the ice cream
until it is a disc. Refreeze for 20 minutes. Run a warm knife around the inside of
the egg ring and remove the ring. Place a disc of ice cream in the centre of each
plate. Place a pear on top of each disc of ice cream.

Ladle chocolate sauce over the top of each pear and serve.

4 cups (1 litre/32 fl oz) water

juice of 1 lemon

1¼ cups (310 g/10 oz) sugar

1 cinnamon stick (quill)

2 cloves

4 whole ripe pears

4 scoops vanilla ice cream
(see page 12)

Chocolate Sauce

1 cup (250 ml/8 fl oz)
double (whipping) cream

310 g (10 oz) dark (plain or
semi-sweet) chocolate

2 tablespoons
Poire William Brandy

Coupe Belle Hélène

Peach Melba

⅔ cup (155 g/5 oz) sugar

2 cups (500 ml/16 fl oz) water

1 cinnamon stick (quill)

2 cloves

3–4 fresh ripe freestone peaches

475 g (15 oz) fresh raspberries

⅓ cup (60 g/2 oz) icing (powdered) sugar

3–4 scoops vanilla ice cream (see page 12)

Named after Dame Nellie Melba, this dessert is the second of the two famous ice cream treats created by Auguste Escoffier, a chef who had as great a passion for desserts as he did for the opera and its stars.

Place the sugar, water, cinnamon sticks and cloves in a large saucepan and bring to the boil. Immerse the peaches in the liquid, and allow it to return to a simmer. Simmer for 10 minutes, then carefully remove the peaches. Let them cool for several minutes, then take a small knife and carefully peel them.

Raspberry Purée

Blend the raspberries in a food processor until they form a smooth paste. Press the purée through a fine sieve or muslin cloth to remove the seeds, then mix with the icing sugar.

Allow to sit for 3 to 4 minutes before serving.

To Assemble

Place a scoop of ice cream in the centre of a chilled coupe dish. Use the back of the ice cream scoop to make a hollow in the centre of the ice cream. Place the peach in this hollow. Ladle a small amount of raspberry purée over the peach and serve immediately.

Dark Chocolate Sorbet

This simple recipe will end your meal with a very different flavour experience. Serve with rich chocolate desserts for a real chocolate 'fix'.

It is one of the most truly exquisite recipes ever taught to me. There are some recipes that you simply hate to part with because they are so good, but this is a book of favourites and so I donate this chocolate delight to your repertoire, where I hope it will remain and be handed down for generations.

2 cups (500 ml/16 fl oz) water

1¼ cups (310 g/10 oz) sugar

¾ cup (90 g/3 oz) cocoa powder

1 vanilla pod

1 tablespoon Crème de Cacao

Place the water, sugar, cocoa and vanilla pod in a saucepan and bring to the boil. Boil the mixture rapidly for 4 minutes.

Remove the mixture from the heat and take out the vanilla pod. Scrape its seeds back into the liquid.

Cool the mixture to room temperature. Stir through the crème de cacao.

Place the chocolate liquid in an ice cream machine and churn it until the mixture is frozen. Freeze the mixture until required.

Cassata

Cassata means 'chest' or 'case'. It is a member of the ice cream bombe family and consists of an outer coating of chocolate ice cream which conceals a creamy inner filling of liqueur-soaked fruits and vanilla ice cream. Decorations can be as simple as Chocolate Curls (see page 125) or as elaborate as you can imagine, with chocolate butterflies, cream piping and other decorations.

Most importantly, this dessert should be served on its own, as a light, but tasty, summer treat.

Place the fruits and the orange and lemon zest in a bowl and cover with the brandy. Leave overnight to soak.

Place 2 cups (500 ml/16 fl oz) of cream in a saucepan and heat until it boils. Meanwhile, in a bowl, whisk the egg yolks and sugar. Whisk the boiled cream into the egg yolk mixture. Return the mixture to the saucepan. Stir the mixture over gentle heat until it coats the back of a spoon. Remove the saucepan from the heat and let the mixture cool.

Whip the remaining 1 cup (250 ml/8 fl oz) of cream and fold this and the soaked fruits into the cooled mixture. Freeze the mixture in its bowl for several hours, stirring or beating every 1 to 2 hours as it hardens.

To Assemble

Line a 1 litre (32 fl oz) round stainless steel bowl or bombe mould with the chocolate ice cream. Refreeze this. Then fill the mould with the cassata filling, cover it with a sheet of plastic wrap (cling film) or foil and freeze it overnight.

Turn the cassata out of its mould and cut into wedges to serve.

Sauce

Place the water and sugar in a saucepan and bring to the boil. Boil until the mixture begins to turn a light golden brown around the edges. Add the remaining ingredients and stir well. Let the sauce cool before serving.

310 g (10 oz) chocolate ice cream (see page 12 or page 15)

1 cup (155 g/5 oz) mixed dried fruit

30 g (1 oz) chopped glacé (candied) cherries

60 g (2 oz) chopped glacé (candied) pineapple

60 g (2 oz) chopped dried apricots

juice and finely grated zest of 1 orange

juice and finely grated zest of 1 lemon

½ cup (125 ml/4 fl oz) brandy

3 cups (750 ml/24 fl oz) double (whipping) cream

4 egg yolks

½ cup (125 g/4 oz) sugar

Following pages: Blueberry Yoghurt Mousse Cups, page 50

MOUSSES

These desserts are easy and relatively fuss free to produce, and vary enormously: they can be heavy or light, rich or subtle.

You can change their flavours simply by substituting different fruit pastes and purées.

Oeufs A La Neige

These delicacies are among the lightest desserts you can make.
The name means 'snow eggs'. They are also known as Iles Flotantes, 'floating
islands', which perhaps best describes them. They are in fact light balls or quenelles
of meringue which are poached in milk and served on a Crème Anglaise.

This very classic dessert has been served to perfection in many restaurants,
but not in all. I now include this as my favourite test of skill for apprentices. I leave
them alone to make it. They often think it is going to be very easy — to some it is,
but others struggle to get even close to the real dessert.

2 cups (500 ml/16 fl oz) milk

1¼ cups (310 g/10 oz) sugar

1 vanilla bean

5 egg whites

Place the milk, ¼ cup (60 g/2 oz) of sugar and the vanilla bean in a low-sided saucepan or frying pan and bring to the boil. Reduce the heat and continue to simmer the milk.

In a bowl, whisk the egg whites until soft peaks form. Slowly add 1 cup (250 g/8 oz) of sugar, still whisking. Continue whisking until all the sugar is dissolved and the whites hold stiff peaks.

Place tablespoon amounts of the meringue in the simmering milk. Turn each meringue over and over for 3 to 4 minutes, until it is set firm.

Remove the meringues carefully, using a slotted spoon, place each straight on a plate or in a bowl of Vanilla Anglaise (see page 117), and serve immediately.

Serves 4

Zabaglione

Many people are scared of making desserts because they think it involves
a lot of time and a lot of expensive ingredients. But, as this Italian dessert shows,
many desserts consist of few ingredients and are relatively easy to produce.

6 egg yolks

¾ cup (185 g/6 oz) sugar

¾ cup (185 ml/6 fl oz) Marsala

ground cinnamon, for dusting

In a large bowl, whisk together the egg yolks and sugar, using a large balloon whisk. Stir in the Marsala.

Place the bowl in a bain-marie or over a pan of hot water and whisk vigorously and continuously, keeping the sides of the bowl clean. The zabaglione is sufficiently cooked when it clings to the whisk when the whisk is raised from the bowl.

Pour the zabaglione into glass goblets and dust the top with cinnamon. Refrigerate until served (at least 1 hour). You can also pour the zabaglione into a loaf tin, freeze it and serve it in slices.

Serve with desserts or over fresh fruits.

NB. For the French variation of the Italian Zabaglione — sabayon — simply substitute champagne for the Marsala.

Serves 4 to 5

Raspberry Crème Brulée

In my career I have seen many recipes for this dessert and just as many experts who know exactly how to make the perfect brulée. Some make thick creams, others light custards and some even make liquefied mixtures which just do not seem to set.

This recipe makes a light, smooth custard, topped with a thin crust of caramel. The caramel should be cooled slightly before serving so that guests must 'crack' through it to the heavenly dessert inside.

1 cup (250 ml/8 fl oz) double (whipping) cream

2 eggs

2 egg yolks

⅔ cup (155 g/5 oz) sugar

1 cup (250 ml/8 fl oz) milk

155 g (5 oz) fresh raspberries

⅓ cup (90 g/3 oz) sugar, extra

4 ramekins (optional)

Preheat the oven to 160°C (320°F).

Place the cream and milk in a saucepan and bring it slowly to the boil.

In a bowl, whisk the eggs, egg yolks and sugar until light and fluffy. Slowly pour the heated cream mixture into the egg yolk mixture and combine them thoroughly.

Evenly distribute the fresh raspberries among 4 ramekins (or small ceramic pots) or pour into one large ovenproof dish. Pour over the cream mixture.

Place the dish/es in a large baking dish (roasting pan). Fill the dish with hot water to halfway up the sides of the dish/es. Place the dish in the oven and cook for 45 to 50 minutes.

Remove the baking dish from the oven. Take the dish/es out of the baking dish and refrigerate them overnight.

Before serving, sprinkle the extra sugar over the top of the dish/es and place them under a hot grill or gas gun (blow torch) until the sugar has caramelised. Then let the brulées cool for 3 to 4 minutes so that the sugar hardens.

Serve with fresh berries.

Serves 4

Chocolate Crème Brulée

3 cups (750 ml/24 fl oz)
double (whipping) cream

finely grated zest of 2 oranges

280 g (9 oz) dark (plain or
semi-sweet) chocolate, chopped

7 egg yolks

¼ cup (60 ml/2 fl oz) Grand
Marnier or orange liqueur

½ cup (90 g/3 oz)
caster (superfine) sugar

6–8 small soufflé ramekins

This is a delicious variation of the classic dessert. I first ate it in France,
very recently.

It is a rich and seductive recipe that will stay at the front of your recipe
catalogue for many years.

Preheat the oven to 200°C (400°F).

Place the cream and the orange zest in a large saucepan. Bring to the boil. Add the chocolate, then take the mixture off the heat. Stir slowly until the chocolate is completely melted and the mixture is smooth.

In a bowl, lightly whisk the egg yolks with the orange liqueur (only whisk until the yolks are broken up). Slowly pour the chocolate mixture into the egg yolks. Stir until combined.

Strain the mixture, then pour it into the soufflé ramekins.

Place the ramekins in a deep baking dish (roasting pan) and fill the dish with cold water to halfway up the sides of the ramekins. Place the baking dish in the oven and bake the brulées for 15 to 20 minutes, or until a skin forms over the top of each brulée.

Remove the baking dish from the oven. Remove the brulées and refrigerate them overnight.

To serve, sprinkle the extra sugar on top of the brulées, then place them under a hot grill or gas gun (blow torch) briefly, until the sugar caramelises. Then let the brulées cool for 3 to 4 minutes so that the sugar hardens. Serve with red berries (a mixture of different kinds of berries works well) and thick cream.

Serves 6 to 8

Passionfruit Bavarois

The main difference between a mousse and a bavarian cream is that the latter, also known simply as 'bavarois', is set using gelatine. Mousses traditionally do not use any setting agent.

My first experience with bavarian creams was on Queensland's Gold Coast, where the following recipe was frequently on our menu, as it offered the sun-bathed diners a light, cold and not-too-filling end to their meals.

The beauty of this recipe is that once the basics have been mastered, the flavour of the recipe can be changed without much trouble at all, as has been done in this recipe. I adore flavours which are light and add a slight tang to the dish, and passionfruit is obviously one of those fruits.

As a child I remember not knowing what the passionfruits were. I would pick them off my father's vine and play baseball with the little round black balls. If I ever hit it correctly my friends and I would get covered in the passionfruit seeds and pulp.

Perhaps it was the reprimanding that we received from these pranks that made me realise the little black fruits were a prized possession in the kitchen! These days I adore them mostly for their flavour and colour — only slightly because they remind me of my father's hand on my bottom!

2½ tablespoons powdered gelatine

5 tablespoons (approximately) cold water

3 cups (750 ml/24 fl oz) milk

1 cup (250 g/8 oz) sugar

6 egg yolks

½ cup (125 ml/4 fl oz) orange juice

3 cups (750 ml/24 fl oz) single (light) cream, whipped

1 cup (250 g/8 oz) passionfruit pulp

10–12 Dariole moulds (optional)

Place the gelatine in a small bowl and cover with enough cold water to soak it up (about 5 tablespoons).

Place the milk in a saucepan and bring it slowly to the boil.

In a large mixing bowl, whisk the sugar and egg yolks until light and fluffy. Slowly pour the boiling milk into the egg yolk mixture, whisking continuously, then add the soaked gelatine. Stir until the gelatine has dissolved.

Fold in the orange juice and place the custard mixture in the refrigerator. Stir occasionally so that it does not set solid. Let it cool until it is cold to the touch (30 to 40 minutes).

Whip the cream until it forms soft peaks. Fold the cream and the passionfruit pulp into the cooled custard, then pour immediately into one large container, or the Dariole moulds.

Refrigerate for 2 hours, or until firmly set.

Serves 10 to 12

Vanilla and Coffee Bavarois

This is an extension of the original bavarois. Your guests will love the surprise when they bite into their vanilla bavarois and find the rich coffee centre hidden in this old-fashioned cream dessert.

If this recipe is a success, you can make try other similar ones simply by changing the flavour of either the first or second amount of bavarois. Have fun combining different colours and taste sensations!

1 tablespoon powdered gelatine

2 cups (500 ml/16 fl oz) milk

1 vanilla pod

3 egg yolks

½ cup (125 g/4 oz) sugar

2 cups (500 ml/16 fl oz) single (light) cream, whipped

1 tablespoon instant coffee granules

1 tablespoon cold water

5–6 Dariole moulds

In a small bowl, soak the gelatine in about 5 tablespoons of cold water.

Place the milk and the vanilla pod in a saucepan. Bring slowly to the boil.

In a large bowl, whisk the sugar and egg yolks until light and fluffy.

Slowly pour the boiling milk into the egg yolk mixture, whisking continuously. Return the mixture to the saucepan and return the saucepan to the heat. Heat the mixture gently, stirring continuously, until it thickens slightly.

Remove the mixture from the heat and add the soaked gelatine. Stir until the gelatine has dissolved. Strain the mixture and remove the vanilla pod. Cut the vanilla pod open and scrape out the seeds into the custard mixture.

Cool the custard mixture in the refrigerator, stirring occasionally to make sure it does not set solid. Let it cool until it is cold to the touch (about 30 minutes).

Lightly whip the cream until it forms soft peaks. Fold the cream into the cooled custard.

Reserve 1½ cups of the mixture in a small bowl. Pour the rest of the mixture into the Dariole moulds. Make sure they are no more than three-quarters full.

Dissolve the coffee granules in the water. (Make the mixture as strong as you like it). Mix the coffee mixture into the reserved bavarois mix. Let both mixtures sit for 5 minutes (out of the refrigerator).

Pour the coffee mixture into a small piping (pastry) bag (see page 126). Use the nozzle of the piping bag to press the coffee mixture into the centre of each bavarois.

Refrigerate the bavarois for 2 to 3 hours, or overnight, to finish setting. Turn the bavarois out (the coffee mixture will be in the middle) and serve with Chocolate Sauce (see page 114) and a light, plain Vanilla Anglaise (see page 117). Use a spoon to place several dots of chocolate sauce in the anglaise. Then, using a knife or a toothpick, run through each dot, joining them up to make a heart shape. Also serve with fresh berries.

Serves 5 to 6

Vanilla and Coffee Bavarois

Crème Caramel

1¼ cups (310 g/10 oz) sugar

¾ cup (185 ml/6 fl oz) water

1 teaspoon liquid glucose
(corn syrup)

4 eggs

2 egg yolks

⅓ cup (90 g/3 oz) sugar

1½ cups (375 ml/12 fl oz) milk

4–5 Dariole moulds or ramekins

Perhaps because I have made so many of these in my career, I respect this dessert for its true self; simple, yet easy to ruin if the caramel is overcooked or the custard is cooked at too high a temperature (bubbles form around its edge). If you are careful with this recipe, a delicious Crème Caramel will result.

Preheat the oven to 135°C (260°F).

Place the sugar, water and glucose in a saucepan and slowly bring to the boil. Boil until the sugar mix becomes a light golden brown colour (has caramelised).

Pour some caramel into each mould or ramekin, so it covers the base of each mould/ramekin to a depth of 2 to 3 mm (⅛ in). Let the caramel harden.

In a bowl, lightly whisk the eggs, egg yolks and sugar until light and creamy. Slowly add the milk and whisk until it is incorporated. Let the mixture rest in the refrigerator for 20 to 30 minutes.

Fill the caramel-based moulds/ramekins with the mixture.

Place the moulds/ramekins in a large baking dishy (roasting pan) and fill the dish with warm water to halfway up the sides of the moulds or ramekins. Place the baking dish in the oven and bake the crème caramels for 35 to 40 minutes, or until they are firm.

Take the baking tray out of the oven, and remove the crème caramels. Refrigerate the crème caramels overnight. To unmould, first run a sharp knife around the inside of each mould/ramekin to loosen the custard. Place a plate, upside down, on top of the mould/ramekin. Turn the plate and mould/ramekin upside down together and shake lightly. The crème caramel should drop from the mould onto the plate, with the caramel sauce spreading over the top.

Serves 4 to 5

Variation: Crème Beau Rivage

In one of my last positions in England as pastrychef, I worked with one of the world's largest contract catering firms.

I had never heard of Crème Beau Rivage when I was handed a recipe for it and told the Managing Director wanted to take this home for his wife's dinner. Halfway through production I clicked that something was not right. I took the recipe to management to ask where they had found such a mistake-ridden recipe, only to find them all crying with laughter.

Make the same custard mixture as above, but whisk 225 g (7 oz) of fresh praline (finely ground) into it. Pour the mixture into 5 or 6 buttered moulds or ramekins, or one large mould. Cook as for Crème Caramel and, again, chill overnight before unmoulding. After unmoulding, serve topped with fresh whipped cream and a sprinkle of extra praline.

Petit Pots Au Chocolat

Everybody (almost!) loves chocolate. These easy-to-make and relatively fuss-free chocolate pots are made from a recipe I picked up on my travels through France.

5 eggs, separated

¼ cup (60 g/2 oz) sugar

250 g (8 oz) dark (plain or semi-sweet) chocolate, melted

2 tablespoons Grand Marnier

zest of 1 orange

In a large bowl, whisk the egg whites until stiff peaks form. Slowly add the sugar, and continue whisking until the sugar is dissolved.

In another bowl, stir the egg yolks with the melted chocolate, then add the Grand Marnier and orange zest. Mix together well.

Fold the whisked egg whites through the chocolate mixture. Pour the mixture into 6 to 8 small ramekins or cups and refrigerate for 2 to 3 hours, or until firm.

Serves 6 to 8

Petits Pots Au Chocolat with Cream

I often vary the chocolate flavours and have several flavours of chocolate pots to serve at once. These are a little richer and heavier than the previous recipe — for the true sinners!

1¼ cups (310 ml/10 fl oz) double (whipping) cream

4 eggs, separated, at room temperature

185 g (6 oz) dark, (plain or semi-sweet) chocolate, melted

zest of 1 orange

6 Dariole moulds or ramekins

In a bowl, semi-whip the cream (to soft peak stage), then let it sit for 10 to 15 minutes, to reach room temperature.

In another bowl, whip the egg whites until they form stiff peaks.

In a small, warm bowl, stir the chocolate and the egg yolks.

Fold the chocolate mixture quickly through the cream. When completely combined, fold in the egg whites and the orange zest.

Pour into one large or 6 individual moulds or ramekins and place in the refrigerator for 2 to 3 hours, or until set.

Serve with fresh fruits.

Serves 6

Crème Chiboust

I first made this delight on a weekend trip to Paris to work in a true French pâtisserie, organised for me by an old Executive chef friend. Crème Chiboust was the only thing I was allowed to put my talents to, however, and that only after I had sworn I would never repeat the recipe to another human being. This recipe is very close to that original recipe; there are only a few changes to add my own flavour and taste.

Crème Chiboust is a light dessert which is a cross between a mousse, a meringue and a cream, and nobody ever really knows what it is made from or indeed how it is made. This light mousse or frozen crème can be served on top of fresh fruits, or as an accompaniment to any other dessert. Traditionally the top is glazed using a gas gun (blow torch) or grill to give a caramelised crust which must be broken through to enjoy the soft cream.

2 level teaspoons gelatine

¼ cup (60 ml/2 fl oz) water

⅔ cup (155 ml/5 fl oz) orange juice

½ cup (125 ml/4 fl oz) single (light) cream

4 tablespoons caster (superfine) sugar

60 g (2 oz) cornflour (cornstarch)

6 egg yolks

6 egg whites

1 cup (225 g/7 oz) caster (superfine) sugar, extra

¼ cup (60 ml/2 fl oz) water, extra

Place the gelatine and the water in a small bowl. Stand the bowl in a pan of hot water to dissolve the gelatine.

Meanwhile, place the orange juice and cream in a saucepan and bring to the boil. In a bowl, whisk together the sugar, cornflour and egg yolks, then pour in the hot cream and orange juice, whisking until combined. Return this mixture to the saucepan and cook over a low heat, stirring continuously, until thickened. Let it cool slightly, then stir in the dissolved gelatine. Let the mixture cool again, but keep stirring to prevent it becoming completely hard or lumpy.

Place the extra sugar and extra water in a small saucepan and bring to the boil. Cook to 130°C (266°F) on a sugar thermometer. Be careful not to overheat the sugar, or it will caramelise. (If you do not have a small saucepan or are not having much luck with your syrup, double the quantities of water and sugar: make a double batch, but only use half.)

Beat the egg whites until stiff peaks form, then slowly add the hot syrup. Beat until the mixture is cold. Then gently fold the egg white mixture, by hand, into the cooled custard.

Line a 7 x 20 x 7 cm (3 x 8 x 3 in) terrine mould with plastic wrap (cling film). Pour the Crème Chiboust into the lined mould, levelling off the surface.

Place the Crème Chiboust in the freezer and leave overnight.

Run a hot knife around the inside of the mould, then remove it.

To serve, cut the frozen Crème Chiboust into slices, and place on top of fresh fruit salad or on the side of any dessert. Place the Crème Chiboust slices under a gas gun (blow torch) or grill for 30 to 40 seconds so that they grill golden brown on top. Serve your dessert immediately so the Crème Chibousts are not completely melted.

Crème Chiboust can also be used (frozen or chilled) as a filling for cakes and pastries such as profiteroles, éclairs and Gâteau Saint Honoré.

Serves 10

Crème Chiboust

Chocolate Marquise

These two rich, luscious and flavoursome mousses combine to make any dessert plate look spectacular. I first made this recipe in Taunton, England, where it was given to me by the pastrychef of the Castle Hotel.

White Chocolate Mousse

2 teaspoons powdered gelatine

1½ tablespoons water

1½ tablespoons liquid glucose (corn syrup)

3 egg yolks

250 g (8 oz) white chocolate, melted

2 cups (500 ml/16 fl oz) double (whipping) cream, softly whipped

Dark Chocolate Mousse

2 teaspoons powdered gelatine

1½ tablespoons water

1½ tablespoons liquid glucose (corn syrup)

3 egg yolks

250 g (8 oz) dark (plain or semi-sweet) chocolate, melted

finely grated zest of 2 oranges

2 cups (500 ml/16 fl oz) double (whipping) cream, softly whipped

Make the White Chocolate Mousse first.

In a saucepan, soak the gelatine in the water. Add the glucose. Melt it by placing the saucepan over a low heat.

Whisk the egg yolks into the heated gelatine/glucose mixture, then add the melted chocolate.

Pour the mixture into the softly whipped cream, stirring quickly to blend.

Follow the same procedure for the Dark Chocolate Mousse, adding the orange zest last. Fold through the zest so that it is evenly distributed.

Use a 30 x 9 x 8 cm (12 x 3½ x 3 in) loaf tin or terrine mould. Sit the tin/mould on an angle (egg cartons make a good support) and pour in the white chocolate mixture. Place the tin/mould in the refrigerator for 30 to 40 minutes, or until the mousse is firm. Then set the tin/mould upright and pour in the dark chocolate mixture. Refrigerate for 2 to 3 hours, then slice thinly and serve.

Serves 6 to 8

Mocha Custards

When you are a pastrychef you never rest when you go out to lunch or dinner; you are always trying to see not only what your dessert is going to look like before it is served to you but also what everybody else is having.

On holidays in Hawaii once, in a situation just like this, I had been served my dessert but saw a dessert being served on another table. It did not look spectacular, but the lady's face shone when she tasted it so I knew it was good. I ordered a second dessert, much to the surprise to the waiting staff, and found it to be the deliciously smooth and flavoursome treat I thought it would be.

If coffee in desserts is not to your liking, the amount in this recipe can be reduced, or omitted. Those who adore coffee and chocolate desserts such as this one, though, can go even further by adding a coffee-flavoured sauce. The amount of coffee flavouring in the dessert can be increased, as well.

3 eggs

3 egg yolks

30 g (1 oz) sugar

½ cup (125 ml/4 fl oz) single (light) cream

90 g (3 oz) dark (plain or semi-sweet) chocolate

2 teaspoons instant coffee granules

Chocolate Curls (see page 123), for decoration

icing (powdered) sugar, for dusting

6 ramekins

Preheat the oven to 180°C (350°F).

In a bowl, whisk the eggs, egg yolks and sugar until creamy.

Place the cream in a saucepan and bring it to the boil. Remove the cream from the heat and add the chocolate, stirring until it is completely melted. Add the coffee granules and whisk until they are dissolved.

Pour the hot liquid over the beaten eggs. Stir until combined well.

Pour the mixture into the ramekins and place the ramekins in a baking dish (roasting pan). Fill this with enough water to reach halfway up the sides of the ramekins.

Bake the mocha custards for 35 to 40 minutes, or until firm.

Remove the baking dish from the oven, take out the ramekins and refrigerate them overnight.

Serve cold with fresh cream, chocolate curls and a light dusting of icing sugar, or with Chocolate Sauce (see page 114).

Serves 6

Avocado Mousse

Many people would never contemplate using avocados in a dessert, but with no savoury flavour, and a consistency which lends itself to a sweet mousse anyway, they make a delicious (if unusual!) end to a meal.

2 ripe avocados

⅓ cup (60 g/2 oz) icing (powdered) sugar

juice and zest of 1 orange

juice and zest of 1 lemon

⅓ cup (90 ml/3 fl oz) single (light) cream

2 egg whites

6 teaspoons sugar

Cut each avocado in half, remove its central nut and scoop out the flesh.

Place the avocado flesh, icing sugar, and orange and lemon juice and zest in a blender. Blend quickly, until smooth. Add the cream and blend again quickly. The cream should be only just combined, but the mixture must be smooth and creamy in texture.

Place the avocado mixture in a bowl.

In another bowl, whisk the egg whites until they form stiff peaks. Slowly drizzle the sugar into the stiff egg whites. Whisk until the sugar is dissolved.

Fold the egg whites into the avocado mixture and spoon the mousse into serving dishes.

Serve immediately.

Serves 3 to 4

Brown Sugar Flummery

During primary school our class had an American exchange teacher for several months. He gave us several of his mother's favourite recipes, one of which was a deep-dish pumpkin pie which I still dream about, another of which was this Brown Sugar Flummery. After almost 20 years, this dessert is still a sensation and I am happy to be passing on the recipe. As Mr Schoolan told me then, when I was eight or nine, 'Never hold on to the recipes that mean everything to you — make somebody else happy by giving them the food you love.'

90 g (3 oz) unsalted butter

1 cup (185 g/6 oz) brown sugar

625 ml (20 fl oz, 2½ cups) milk

⅛ teaspoon cinnamon

3 eggs, separated

15 g (½ oz) powdered gelatine

2 tablespoons water

Heat the butter in a saucepan until it melts. Add the brown sugar and stir. Continue heating the mixture until a caramel is formed. Still on the heat, slowly add the milk, then the cinnamon. Keep stirring until completely combined. Remove the saucepan from the heat.

In a bowl, lightly whisk the egg yolks. Pour half the milk liquid over the egg yolks, whisking continuously. When combined, add the egg yolk mixture to the rest of the milk mixture. Heat gently until the mixture thickens and coats the back of a spoon. Take the mixture off the heat.

Dissolve the gelatine in the water and stir this into the mixture. Let the mixture cool completely, but do not let it set firm.

In another bowl, whisk the egg whites until stiff peaks form. Fold them through the mixture. Pour the flummery into 4 coupe glasses. Refrigerate for 1 to 2 hours, or until set.

Serves 4

Avocado Mousse (right) and Brown Sugar Flummery (left)

Lemon Snow

1 cup (250 g/8 oz) sugar

2 cups (500 ml/16 fl oz) boiling water

juice and finely grated zest of 2 lemons

2 tablespoons cornflour (cornstarch)

2 egg whites

This simple dessert is a favourite for two reasons; I adore the flavour of citrus because it keeps a dessert light and luscious while adding a slight tartness to the taste. Secondly, because the dessert is so light, it can be served after any meal, or for late afternoon summer parties, or served individually for afternoon tea.

Place the sugar and water in a saucepan and bring to the boil.

In a bowl, mix the cornflour with the lemon juice and zest until smooth. When the syrup boils, remove it from the heat and whisk in the cornflour mixture. Return the mixture to the heat and stir continuously until it boils again. Take it off the heat and let it cool.

In another bowl, whisk the egg whites until they form stiff peaks. Fold the egg whites through the cooling lemon mixture. Refrigerate the mixture until it is cold (about 1 hour), then serve.

Serves 4 to 6

Tangy Lemon Cream

I have adored the flavour of citrus fruits since my early days in the pastry kitchen. The lemon gives a wonderful bite to this cream. You can serve it in small spoonfuls beside afternoon tea cakes, for summer high teas, or on its own as a dinner dessert.

20 g (¾ oz) powdered gelatine

⅓ cup (90 ml/3 fl oz) cold water

⅓ cup (90 ml/3 fl oz) boiling water

1 cup (250 g/8 oz) sugar

1¼ cups (310 ml/10 fl oz) lemon juice

finely grated zest of 1 lemon

1 cup (250 ml/8 fl oz) double (whipping) cream, whipped

4 egg whites

Sprinkle the gelatine over the cold water and let it soak.

Place the boiling water in a medium-sized bowl. Dissolve the soaked gelatine in the boiling water.

Mix the sugar and the lemon juice and zest into the gelatine mixture, stirring until the sugar has dissolved. Chill the mixture until it thickens slightly.

In another bowl, whisk the egg whites until stiff peaks form.

Fold the whipped cream through the thickening lemon mixture, then fold in the egg whites.

Pour the mixture into 4 to 6 individual ramekins or serving glasses. Refrigerate until firm (1 to 2 hours).

Serve with fresh cream.

Serves 4 to 6

Strawberry Mousse

*I first found this recipe when I was 15, and I have used it professionally
and at home ever since. No matter what time of year it is, and what fruits are in
season, you can use this recipe — it can be adapted to any berry flavour.*

Wash the strawberries and remove their stalks. Purée the berries with the sugar
in a food processor.

Soak the gelatine in the cold water. Place the lemon juice and the extra water
in a saucepan and heat. Add the soaked gelatine and stir, off the heat, until it is
dissolved. Let the mixture cool slightly, then add it to the strawberry purée. Mix
it in quickly and thoroughly.

Fold the whipped cream into the mixture just before the mixture sets.

Pour the mousse into 4 to 6 ramekins and refrigerate it for 1 to 2 hours, until
it is set. Then decorate the mousses, or just turn them out of their moulds.

Serve with Marinated Berries (see page 113) and fresh cream.

Serves 4 to 6

500 g (1 lb) fresh strawberries

½ cup (90 g/3 oz)
icing (powdered) sugar

1 tablespoon powdered gelatine

4 tablespoons cold water
(for soaking the gelatine)

juice of ½ lemon

¼ cup (60 ml/2 fl oz)
water, extra

1 cup (250 ml/8 fl oz) double
(whipping) cream, whipped

Marinated Berries
(see page 113), for serving

Berry Heaven

This rich fantasy dessert should be served after a light meal — your guests will appreciate having enough room left for it! Served with a chilled glass of muscat, this dessert will make you a hit with whomever you serve it to.

An apprentice of mine invented this dessert by mistake. She prepared a chocolate cake mixture but forgot to put in the flour. She placed the mixture in the refrigerator and when I tasted it, I decided to just fold through the cream and berries and serve it as a very rich mousse.

Success was ours and the recipe has stayed in my recipe book for years.

6 egg yolks

½ cup (90 g/3 oz) icing (powdered) sugar

250 g (8 oz) unsalted butter, softened

5 tablespoons cocoa powder, sifted

155 g (5 oz) dark (plain or semi-sweet) chocolate, melted

1¼ cups (310 ml/10 fl oz) double (whipping) cream

½ cup (90 g/3 oz) icing (powdered) sugar, extra

225 g (7 oz) fresh raspberries

In a bowl, whisk the egg yolks and icing sugar until thick, light and fluffy.

In another bowl, whip the butter and cocoa together until light, fluffy and very soft.

Whisk the chocolate into the egg yolk mixture, then add the butter mixture. Combine thoroughly.

In another bowl, lightly whip the cream with the extra icing sugar.

Add the cream to the mixture. Just before it is all folded in, add the raspberries and combine.

Pour the mixture into 8 fluted glasses and chill for 1 hour before serving.

Serves 8

Raspberry Fool

I was once asked what the difference was between a 'fool' and a 'whip' — at the time, I could not think what it was! A fool is lightened with whipped cream only, whereas a whip is lightened with egg whites. So if you add a little egg white to this recipe, you can make a 'berry fool whip'. Either way, this simple dessert tastes just delicious. It is a great standby, easily made using either fresh or frozen berries.

625 g (20 oz) fresh or frozen raspberries

1 cup (185 g/6 oz) icing (powdered) sugar

2 cups (500 ml/16 fl oz) double (whipping) cream, whipped

Place the raspberries and sugar in a food processor and purée.

Fold through the whipped cream and pour the mixture into coupe glasses or 4 to 6 champagne flutes. Refrigerate for 1 to 2 hours before serving.

Serve with fresh fruit.

Serves 4 to 6

Berry Heaven (left) and Raspberry Fool (right)

Blueberry Yoghurt Mousse Cups

Mousse

30 g (1 oz) powdered gelatine

4 tablespoons orange juice

1 cup (250 ml/8 fl oz)
blueberry purée

½ cup (125 g/4 oz,)sugar

1 cup (250 ml/8 fl oz)
plain yoghurt

1 cup (250 ml/8 fl oz) double
(whipping) cream, whipped

White Biscuit Mixture

⅔ cup (125 g/4 oz)
icing (powdered) sugar

1 cup (125 g/4 oz)
plain (all-purpose) flour

3 egg whites

90 g (3 oz) unsalted butter,
melted

Chocolate Biscuit Mixture

6 egg whites

1 cup (185 g/6 oz)
icing (powdered) sugar

½ cup (60 g/2 oz)
plain (all-purpose) flour

¼ cup (30 g/1 oz) cocoa powder

75 g (2½ oz) unsalted butter,
melted

20–30 whole fresh blueberries

10–12 Dariole moulds

This dessert comes all the way from England. It was adored by guests at Hambleton Hall in Leicestershire, where we served it with marinated mixed berries and tuile biscuits. This variation on the original light and tasty summer mousse is sensational, with its striped biscuit collar. The recipe was first created as a sample while tendering for international airline catering contracts.

In a small bowl, sprinkle the powdered gelatine over the orange juice and leave it to soak.

In a saucepan, heat the blueberry purée and sugar to a gentle simmer. Remove the saucepan from the heat and add the soaked gelatine. Let the mixture cool.

Fold the yoghurt through the cooled blueberry mixture, then fold through the whipped cream. When completely combined, refrigerate the mousse until it is required, but do not let the mixture become firm.

Vanilla Biscuit

Preheat the oven to 180°C (350°F) and line a baking tray (sheet) with baking paper (parchment).

In a bowl, whisk the egg whites with the icing sugar until the sugar is incorporated. Add the flour and mix. Let the batter rest for 10 to 15 minutes, then fold through the melted butter.

Refrigerate the mixture for 30 to 40 minutes, until it is firm.

Chocolate Biscuit

In a bowl, whisk the egg whites with the icing sugar until the sugar is incorporated. Add the flour and the sifted cocoa and mix. Let the batter rest for 10 to 15 minutes, then fold through the melted butter.

Refrigerate the mixture for 30 to 40 minutes, until it is firm.

Biscuit Collars

Using a piping bag, pipe a thin layer of the white biscuit mixture randomly onto the lined baking tray. Place the tray in the freezer for 10 to 15 minutes, or until the rows are frozen solid.

Remove the tray from the freezer and quickly spread the chocolate biscuit mixture over the top of the white mixture.

Bake the sheet of mixture for 8 to 10 minutes, or until it is firm to the touch on top but not brown (if it browns, the biscuit will be too crisp).

Remove the sheet from the oven and let the biscuit cool slightly before cutting it into strips 10 cm (4 in) long and 5 cm (2 in) wide.

Quickly place one strip inside each of the Dariole moulds, making certain that the striped side faces outwards. Make sure that the two ends of the strip overlap a little, so that the mousse will not run out.

Pour the mousse mixture into the prepared moulds, half filling them. Drop 3 or 4 whole blueberries into the centre of each mould, then pour in more mousse. Refrigerate the dessert for 2 to 3 hours before unmoulding and serving with berries.

Serves 10 to 12

Nectarine Velvet

The often-forgotten flavours of the nectarine are highlighted in this delicious, smooth dessert. Served in a biscuit basket or with light Shortbread Biscuits (see page 122), this is a wonderful spring or summer mousse. If you freeze it and stir it every five minutes during its freezing, it will also make an excellent nectarine ice cream.

4½ cups (1.125 litres/36 fl oz) water

625 g (20 oz) fresh nectarines

2 cinnamon sticks (quills)

¼ cup (60 g/2 oz) sugar

60 g (2 oz) unsalted butter

5 egg yolks

30 g (1 oz/7 teaspoons) cornflour (cornstarch)

1¼ cups (310 ml/10 fl oz) milk

185 ml (6 fl oz/¾ cup) double (whipping) cream, whipped

Place 1 litre (32 fl oz) of water in a saucepan and bring it to the boil. Place the nectarines, one at a time, in the water and poach them for 1 to 2 minutes. Carefully remove them, peel them, cut them in half and remove the stones.

In another saucepan, heat the remaining water, cinnamon sticks, sugar and butter until the mixture boils. Add the nectarine halves and place the lid on top. Simmer for 15 to 20 minutes, or until the nectarines are soft.

Remove the cinnamon sticks. Place the hot fruit and syrup in a food processor and purée.

In a bowl, whisk the milk with the cornflour and the egg yolks until you have a smooth liquid. Transfer this mixture to a saucepan and cook it over a low heat, stirring continuously to make sure it does not burn. When the mixture begins to thicken, add the nectarine purée. Continue to cook the mixture, still stirring continuously, for a further 3 to 5 minutes. The mixture should then be thick. Remove the mixture from the heat and let it cool.

When it is cold, fold through the whipped cream.

Serve the Nectarine Velvet in small pastry cases, Chocolate Baskets (see page 122) or as an accompaniment to fresh fruits.

Serves 4 to 6

Rose Petal Mousse with Raspberry Sauce

This is a great conversation-starting dessert. I first tried making desserts with fresh products from the garden when I was guest chef at a flower show. My efforts were rewarded with this recipe, which was remembered long after my appearances. But the rose growers did not know exactly how to take it, as they liked the flowers in their gardens, not in their kitchens!

For best results, use roses of varying colours and with highly perfumed petals, so your guests can enjoy the taste and aroma of your dessert.

2 teaspoons gelatine

1½ tablespoons water

1½ tablespoons liquid glucose (corn syrup)

2 egg yolks

250 g (8 oz) white chocolate, melted

2½ cups (625 ml/20 fl oz) double (whipping) cream, very lightly whipped

zest and juice of 1 lemon

petals of 3 medium roses, different colours, washed

Raspberry Sauce

225 g (7 oz) fresh raspberries, hulled and washed

sugar, to sweeten

2½ tablespoons cold water

In a saucepan, soak the gelatine in the water. Add the glucose, then heat the mixture gently until it melts. Remove the mixture from the heat, then add the egg yolks and whisk quickly and thoroughly to combine.

Stir in the melted chocolate. (If the chocolate mixture has 'tightened', heat it over a low flame to re-melt it.) Stir it into the egg yolk and gelatine mixture, then mix this into the cream by hand. Add the warm mixture immediately to the cream, then add lemon juice and zest and rose petals.

Pour the mixture into a 25 x 30 x 3 cm (10 x 12 x 1¼ in) baking dish (roasting pan) lined with plastic wrap (cling film), and refrigerate until firm (about 1 hour).

Raspberry Sauce

Place raspberries and water in a blender with enough sugar to sweeten. Purée until smooth.

To serve, cut the mousse into 5 cm (2 in) squares, then cut each square in half diagonally to make a triangle. Serve 4 triangles, standing upright, per person, on raspberry sauce and with fresh fruits.

Serves 6 to 8

Rose Petal Mousse

Pear Fool

500 g (1 lb) fresh pears, peeled,
cored and sliced

½ cup (125 g/4 oz) sugar

⅓ cup (90 ml/3 fl oz) water

juice of 1 lemon

1 cup (250 ml/8 fl oz) double
(whipping) cream, whipped

30 ml (1 fl oz) Poire William
brandy

*Of all the fruits available to pastrychefs and home cooks, pears and
stone fruits seem to miss out the most, yet when desserts are made
from these fruits, they are loved.*

*Pears give this fool a light and subtle flavour, making the dessert perfect
for those summer nights when both the chef and the guests have had almost
enough food, but just need a little sweetening up.*

Place the pears in a saucepan with the sugar, water and lemon juice. Cook
slowly until you have a fairly stiff purée. Sieve the purée into a basin and let it
cool thoroughly.

When the purée is cold, fold through the cream and the brandy. Ladle into
glass coupes and smooth the surface level. Refrigerate until set (1 to 2 hours).

Decorate the pear fools with slices of fresh pear which have been sprinkled
with sugar and glazed under the grill.

Serves 6 to 8

Citrus and Semillon Whip

*Dessert or sweet wines are not only the perfect accompaniment for many desserts —
they can also be used in many of them. Use your favourite semillon for this recipe,
and serve the rest of the bottle with the dessert!*

*This dessert is deliciously light and can be served after the heaviest of meals. It is just
as good on summer evenings or for spring picnics, too.*

2 large oranges

4 sugar cubes

5 tablespoons sauterne or
your favourite sweet white
dessert wine

½ cup (125 ml/4 fl oz)
single (light) cream

1 cup (250 ml/8 fl oz)
double (whipping) cream

4–5 tuile cups (see page 120)

Rub the oranges with the sugar cubes to extract the essences, oils and colour.
Then juice the oranges. Place the orange juice, sugar cubes and wine in a bowl.
Let this mixture sit for 1 hour, stirring occasionally to help dissolve the sugar.

Add the cream, and whisk the mixture until it begins to hold soft peaks.

Pour the mixture into Tuile Cups (see page 120) and serve immediately, with
strands of orange zest on top.

Serves 4 to 5

Citrus Mousse

*Citrus fruits are rarely (if ever) unavailable, making this dessert
a godsend when you just cannot think what to cook for a special evening.*

*This recipe was sent to me by a reader of one of my newspaper columns. I have added
the flavours of other citrus fruits to make it a special taste sensation.*

*This mousse could also be made from mandarins, tangerines or grapefruit,
and served with a medley of citrus fruits, making a delightful
summer or spring dessert.*

Place the zest and juice of the lemons, oranges and lime in a saucepan with the sugar and water. Heat until the sugar dissolves.

Soak the gelatine in cold water, then add the gelatine to the citrus syrup. Stir, off the heat, until the gelatine has dissolved. Let the mixture cool.

In a bowl, lightly whip the cream. Fold in the lemon mixture just before it sets. Pour the mousse into 6 moulds which have been very lightly greased with oil. Refrigerate the mousses until they are set (1 to 2 hours).

Simply shake the moulds to release the mousses. If they do not come freely, dip the moulds quickly into warm water and turn them upside down onto the serving plates.

Serve with a medley of citrus segments and fresh cream.

Serves 6

*juice and finely grated zest of
2 lemons*

*juice and finely grated zest of
2 oranges*

*juice and finely grated zest of
1 lime*

1 cup (250 g/8 oz) sugar

⅓ cup (90 ml/3 fl oz) water

1 tablespoon powdered gelatine

*3 cups (750 ml/24 fl oz)
single (light) cream*

PUDDINGS

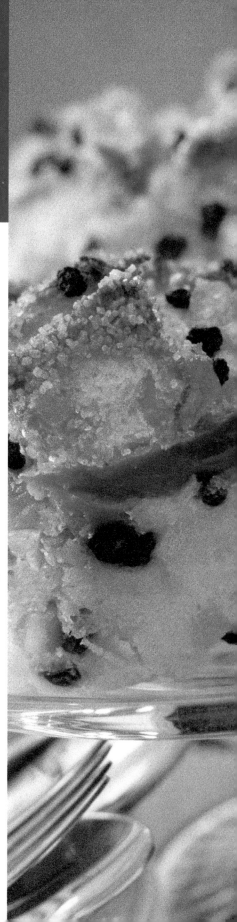

Here are some of the most
wonderful winter comfort foods —
the most popular fruit puddings,
and the tried and true egg-based
puddings born in Europe and
England but now well loved
everywhere.

Some are original recipes, and some
have just a tiny variation that makes
the dish exceptional.

Diplomat Pudding

1/3 cup (60 g/2 oz) currants

1/2 cup (60 g/2 oz) chopped
dried apricots

boiling water

1/3 cup (60 g/2 oz) chopped
glacé (candied) cherries

2 tablespoons chopped
candied angelica

1/3 cup (90 ml/3 fl oz) Kirsch

2 cups (500 ml/16 fl oz)
sour cream

2 cups (500 ml/16 fl oz) milk

6 eggs

2/3 cup (155 g/5 oz) sugar

1/2 génoise sponge,
cut into 1 cm (1/2 in) cubes
(see page 119)

This pudding is quite similar in style to the cabinet pudding, but should be lighter in taste and is flavoured with Kirsch. Diplomat pudding is also very colourful, because of the array of dried fruits used.

When I first made this, during my apprenticeship, I did not know how to poach dried fruits. As I have learnt more, this dessert has just kept getting better! To ensure success, soak the dried fruit in boiling water until the water cools, then drain it. Repeat the process several times. This allows the dried fruit to rejuvenate into plump, moist fruit and soak up the alcohol it is then steeped in, making for a more aromatic and flavour-filled dessert.

Preheat the oven to 150°C (300°F).

Place the currants and dried apricot pieces in a large bowl and cover with boiling water. When the water is cool, drain the fruit. Repeat this process until the fruit is soft and plump. Then place the currants and apricots in a smaller bowl with the cherries and angelica, and pour over the Kirsch. Let it sit, covered, overnight.

In another bowl, whisk the sour cream with the milk, sugar and eggs until combined.

Sprinkle the sponge cubes, and then the chopped cherries, apricots, currants and angelica, into a loaf tin or terrine mould (25 x 10 x 10 cm/10 x 4 x 4 in). Pour over the egg liquid and let the mixture sit for 5 minutes, so the sponge can soak up the liquid.

Place the terrine mould in a large baking dish (roasting pan) half filled with water and bake for 3/4 to 1 hour, or until the custard is set firm.

Cool the pudding in the refrigerator for 2 hours, then cut it into 1 cm (1/2 in) thick slices and serve on Lemon Sauce (see page 115).

Serves 8 to 10

Previous page: Brioche and Butter Pudding, page 68

Eve's Pudding

As with many of the puddings in this book, I first made this in the United Kingdom. At first I thought that the name was a joke played on me by my fellow chefs but they reassured me that indeed this apple-based dessert was named Eve's Pudding because apples were the fruit Eve gave to Adam.

Eve's Pudding is a relative of the French Tarte Tatin and the American Upside Down Cake, but is different enough to warrant inclusion in the list of my favourite pudding recipes.

Preheat the oven to 180°C (350°F).

Place the chopped apples in the base of a deep pie dish and sprinkle them with the demerara sugar.

In a bowl, cream the butter and sugar until light and fluffy. Add the eggs one at a time, beating well after each addition. Add the sifted flour and cocoa powder, spices, baking powder and milk, and mix well. Spread this mixture over the apples and bake for 45 to 50 minutes, or until a knife inserted into the sponge mixture comes out clean.

Remove the pudding from the oven and let it stand for 3 to 4 minutes. Turn the pudding out upside down onto a plate and serve.

Serves 6 to 8

---

3 cooking apples, peeled, cored and chopped finely

185 g (6 oz) unsalted butter

½ cup (125 g/4 oz) demerara sugar

⅔ cup (155 g/5 oz) sugar

3 eggs, beaten

2 cups (250 g/8 oz) plain (all-purpose) flour, sifted

1 teaspoon cocoa powder

½ teaspoon cinnamon

⅛ teaspoon ground cloves

10 g (⅓ oz) baking powder

¼ cup (60 ml/2 fl oz) milk

Chocolate Pudding with a Melting Middle

During my apprenticeship we sampled this dessert with many different types of fillings, but we could never get a better result or response from our customers than when we used plain dark chocolate.

Serve this dessert covered with rich chocolate sauce and clotted cream, and accompanied by a glass of port or muscat, to make a dark, blustery, winter's night that you will never forget.

225 g (7 oz) unsalted butter, softened

1 cup (250 g/8 oz) sugar

225 g (7 oz) dark (plain or semi-sweet) chocolate, melted

6 eggs, separated

1½ cups (185 g/6 oz) plain (all-purpose) flour, sifted

½ teaspoon baking powder

1½ cups (185 g/6 oz) ground (minced) almonds

75 g (2½ oz) dark (plain or semi-sweet) chocolate, preferably in 1 cm (½ in) cubes

8 Dariole moulds (250 ml/ 8 fl oz each)

sugar, for the moulds

In a bowl, cream the butter and sugar until light and fluffy. Add the melted chocolate and combine. Scrape down the sides of the bowl to ensure all the chocolate has been mixed thoroughly. Add the egg yolks, one at a time, and combine well, then add the sifted flour, baking powder and ground almonds.

Whisk the egg whites until stiff peaks form. Carefully fold the egg whites through the chocolate mixture. Place the mixture in an airtight container in the refrigerator for 1 hour.

Preheat the oven to 180°C (350°F).

Lightly brush the Dariole moulds with melted butter. Coat the base and sides of each mould with sugar.

Using a small spoon or spatula, fill each mould with the chilled mixture to a depth of 1 cm (½ in) on the base and around the sides, leaving a small hole in the centre. Put a cube of chocolate in this hole, then seal the mould with more of the chilled mixture. Place the mould on a baking tray (sheet) and bake for 40 to 45 minutes.

When baked, carefully run a knife around the inside of each mould to ease the baked pudding from its container. Unmould the puddings onto plates and serve with Custard (see page 118) or Chocolate Sauce (page 114), or simply dusted with drinking chocolate.

Serves 8

Chocolate Pudding with a Melting Middle

Queen of Puddings

1¼ cups (310 ml/10 fl oz) milk

1¼ cups (310 ml/10 fl oz)
single (light) cream

1 vanilla pod

3 eggs

¼ cup (60 g/2 oz) sugar

310 g (10 oz) sponge pieces,
cut into 1 cm (½ in) cubes

2 tablespoons strawberry jam

2 egg whites

¼ cup (60 g/2 oz) sugar

The base of this dessert is very similar to the Bread and Butter, Diplomat and Cabinet puddings, but the rich jam and meringue topping is decidedly different.

I like these served individually, but for large groups it is much easier to use a large baking dish (roasting pan) and simply serve spoonfuls.

I first ate this dessert in a small English pub in Oakham, called the Finch's Arms. I had eaten and drunk there many a time, as I worked close by, and I was amazed, on this day, that the cook had gone to so much trouble — usually we enjoyed very simple although perfect food; nothing as rich or as tasty as this dessert.

My quizzing of the cook revealed that the day was the Queen's Birthday and that this was the only recipe he knew that even remotely resembled anything royal. This answer had me believing for several years that this dessert was called 'Queen's Pudding'. When reality struck, years later, I was a little upset that my original views were not correct. Although it is unclear who actually invented the Queen of Puddings, I suspect it is called this because, like the great lady herself, it is the 'richest' of its type!

Place the milk, cream and vanilla pod in a saucepan and bring to the boil. Remove from the heat and cool slightly.

In a bowl, whisk the eggs and sugar until completely blended.

Remove the vanilla pod from the saucepan, split it and scrape out the seeds into the milk and cream mixture.

Slowly pour the milk and cream mixture into the egg mixture, whisking continuously. Let the mixture rest for 20 minutes.

Sprinkle the sponge pieces into one large ramekin or 6 individual ramekins. Pour the egg mixture evenly over the sponge. Let the mixture sit for 5 minutes, so the sponge can soak up the liquid. Place the container/s in a baking dish (roasting pan). Pour in enough hot water to reach halfway up the sides of the container/s.

Place the baking dish in the oven and bake until the custard is golden brown and set. Remove the custard and let it cool.

In a bowl, whisk the egg whites to stiff peaks. Slowly sprinkle in the sugar and keep whisking until the sugar is dissolved and a firm meringue has been formed.

Spread the top of the custard/s with the jam and top with the meringue. Return the ramekin/s to the oven for 5 to 8 minutes, or until the meringue is golden brown.

Serves 6 to 8

Cabinet Pudding

This variation of the original dessert was first served to me in the heart of England and has remained a favourite dessert ever since. It is a far cry from the original 18th century dessert, which consisted of dried bread scraps soaked in milk and then set with a mixture of egg and sugar.

Preheat the oven to 150°C (300°F).

Place the orange zest and the sultanas in a basin and pour over the Grand Marnier. Cover and leave for 24 hours.

Place the cream in a saucepan and bring slowly to the boil. Take the cream off the heat and add the chocolate. Stir the mixture until the chocolate is completely melted and combined. Let the mixture cool.

Whisk the eggs and sugar into the chocolate cream, until the sugar has dissolved. Let the mixture rest for 30 minutes.

Spread the soaked sultanas over the base of one large pudding basin or 6 individual 250 ml (8 oz) ramekins, then sprinkle the sponge cubes over the sultanas.

Pour the egg/cream mixture over the sponge and leave it for 5 minutes, so the mixture can soak into the sponge pieces.

Place the pudding bowl or ramekins in a baking tray half filled with warm water, and bake for 35 to 40 minutes, or until a knife inserted into the centre of the dish/es does not reveal any liquid custard.

Serve the individual puddings in their dishes. Serve hot or cold.

Serves 6

finely grated zest of 2 oranges

1⅓ cups (310 g/10 oz) sultanas (golden raisins)

½ cup (125 ml/4 fl oz) Grand Marnier or other orange liqueur

2 cups (500 ml/16 fl oz) single (light) cream

60 g (2 oz) dark (plain or semi-sweet) chocolate, finely chopped

5 eggs

⅓ cup (90 g/3 oz) sugar

3½ cups (225 g/7 oz) fresh chocolate sponge or cake, cut into 1 cm (½ in) cubes

Chocolate Ginger Sponge

125 g (4 oz) unsalted butter,
softened

¼ cup (60 g/2 oz) sugar

30 g (1 oz) raw ginger,
finely grated

5 eggs, separated

60 g (2 oz) dark (plain or
semi-sweet) chocolate, melted

3 tablespoons cocoa powder, sifted

1¼ cups (155 g/5 oz) plain
(all-purpose) flour, sifted

1 teaspoon baking powder

¼ cup (60 g/2 oz) sugar, extra

1½ tablespoons dark rum

icing (powdered) sugar,
for dusting

In one of the few big mistakes I have ever made in the professional kitchen, I once used Jerusalem artichoke in this recipe instead of fresh ginger and wondered why there was very little ginger aroma to the finished products. The guests complimented me on a fine dessert and when they returned a few weeks later, mentioned that I was now putting in a little too much ginger for their liking.

As my mother taught me, 'what the eye does not see the heart does not grieve', so if you ever make the same mistake, just keep it to yourself!

In this recipe I have cut down slightly on the ginger content. If fresh ginger is unavailable, use the dry powder, but the fresh product does give the best results.

Preheat the oven to 180°C (350°F). Grease a 20 cm (8 in) springform cake tin. Line the base with baking paper (parchment).

In a bowl, cream the butter and sugar with the finely grated raw ginger until light and fluffy. Add the egg yolks one at a time, beating well after each addition. Add the melted chocolate, mixing quickly to ensure the chocolate is combined before it hardens. Then add the cocoa powder, sifted flour and baking powder, and combine well.

In another bowl, whisk the egg whites until stiff peaks begin to form. While mixing, gradually add the extra sugar. Continue to whisk until the sugar has dissolved. Fold the egg whites and the rum carefully into the chocolate mixture.

Pour the mixture into the prepared cake pan and bake for 35 to 40 minutes, or until a skewer inserted into the top of the cake comes out clean.

Cool the sponge in the cake tin, then remove it, dust it lightly with icing sugar and serve it warm with Chocolate Sauce (see page 114) spiked with a little fresh ginger.

Serves 8 to 10

Spotted Dick

In my childhood my mother made this delightful English dessert — all too infrequently! I had forgotten this recipe until I began working at the Castle Hotel, Taunton, England, where we made very traditional English meals taste and look exciting for modern diners.

For those who like the flavours of tradition, this recipe is a real winner. For those who like to experiment a little, the currants can be replaced by chocolate chips.

1¼ cups (225 g/7 oz) currants

½ cup (125 ml/4 fl oz) brandy

125 g (4 oz) unsalted butter

⅔ cup (155 g/5 oz) sugar

3 eggs

1¼ cups (225 g/7 oz) plain (all-purpose) flour, sifted

2 teaspoons baking powder

2 tablespoons milk

2 tablespoons golden syrup (treacle), for serving

Place the currants in enough boiling water to cover them. Soak them until the water is cool, then drain. Repeat this process, then place the currants in a fresh bowl, pour over the brandy and steep overnight.

Preheat the oven to 180°C (350°F).

Lightly grease 6 Dariole moulds or ramekins.

In a bowl, cream the butter and sugar until light and fluffy. Add the eggs, one at a time, beating well after each addition. Add the flour, baking powder and milk. Fold in the currants and brandy. Pour the batter into the moulds, filling them just over half full.

Cover the top of each mould/ramekin with aluminium foil. Place them in a deep baking dish (roasting pan). Fill the baking dish with warm water to halfway up the sides of the moulds/ramekins.

Bake for 45 to 50 minutes, or until a skewer inserted into the middle of a pudding comes out clean.

Serve with thick, pure, dairy cream or warmed golden syrup.

Serves 6

Sticky Toffee
and Date Pudding

2½ cups (475 g/15 oz) chopped dried dates

2 cups (500 ml/16 fl oz) water

125 g (4 oz) unsalted butter

1½ cups (375 g/12 oz) sugar

4 eggs

3 cups (375 g/12 oz) plain (all-purpose) flour

2 teaspoons vanilla essence

2 teaspoons baking powder

2 teaspoons bicarbonate of soda (baking soda)

In my first position as a pastry chef in England I was asked to cook a sticky toffee pudding similar to that of Francis Coulson of the Sharrow Bay Hotel in the Lake District. Instead of mimicking his efforts I asked him personally for his recipe. The dish is found all around the world, served with various sauces and called various names. His original recipe is now finally in print, exactly as it was given to me.

Preheat the oven to 180°C (350°F). Grease two 28 x 20 x 6 cm (11 x 8 x 2½ in) baking dishes (roasting pans).

Place the dates and water in a saucepan and boil until the dates are soft and the liquid has almost disappeared.

In a bowl, cream the butter and sugar until very light and very pale. Add the eggs and beat well. The mixture should become very light and almost liquid. Add the flour, baking powder and vanilla essence and beat well.

Add the bicarbonate of soda to the dates. Let the mixture bubble, then pour it into the sponge mixture. Mix well.

Pour the mixture into the baking dishes and bake for 40 to 45 minutes, until the sponge is well risen and brown).

Serve with Treacle or Butterscotch Sauce (see page 115).

Serves 6 to 8

Sticky Toffee and Date Pudding

Brioche and Butter Pudding

3–4 slices of 1–2-day-old brioche

2–3 tablespoons unsalted butter

2 tablespoons
mixed (candied) peel

2 tablespoons currants

1¼ cups (310 ml/10 fl oz) milk

2 eggs

2 egg yolks

¼ cup (60 g/2 oz) sugar

5 teaspoons raw sugar

This dessert was originally made by peasants in England. They mixed what bread scraps they had with milk and set it in a mixture of eggs and milk or water. Eventually the mixture was sweetened, and in those households that could afford them, other ingredients were added.

Bread and butter pudding is an English institution and it is from this base that such other delicacies as Diplomat, Cabinet and Queen of Puddings developed. This modernised version of the classic simply enriches the original recipe by using French brioche. Bread can still be used if brioche is unavailable.

Preheat the oven to 160°C (300°F).

Spread the brioche slices with the butter, then chop them into pieces and spread the pieces among 4 to 6 ramekins or Dariole moulds. Sprinkle over the mixed peel and currants, then continue layering brioche pieces and dried fruit until both are used up.

In a bowl, whisk the milk, eggs and sugar until combined. Pour the milk mixture over the brioche and dried fruits in the ramekins/moulds. Sprinkle a teaspoon of raw sugar over each pudding.

Place the ramekins or moulds in a baking dish (roasting pan). Pour enough hot water into the tray to reach halfway up the sides of the ramekins/moulds.

Bake for 35 to 40 minutes, until the custard is golden brown on top and has set firm. Serve warm in the ramekins, or let the puddings cool and unmould them. Serve the puddings on their own, or with fresh cream, or with a fruit purée, after a traditional Sunday roast.

Serves 4 to 6

Steamed Sponge Pudding

Nothing beats a nice, light, steamed pudding, and this recipe is definitely that.

*If there is one truly great thing about growing older, it is that our memories of childhood become more dear to us with every passing day. As life becomes more confused and hectic, I often find myself looking at photos or simply recalling my untroubled youth, where the toughest problem in life seemed to be who was actually going to get the beaters to lick after Mum had made dessert.
This was a nightly ritual in our family during winter, where it was bitterly cold outside but warm through to the heart inside.
There were fine gastronomic delights to enjoy each evening.*

2 tablespoons unsalted butter,
for greasing

250 g (8 oz) unsalted butter

1 cup (250 g/8 oz) sugar

4 eggs

3 cups (375 g/12 oz)
plain (all-purpose) flour, sifted

1 tablespoon baking powder

¼ cup (60 ml/2 fl oz) milk

Of all the nights and all the winter meals I can remember, my memories seem to most frequently return to those nights where steamed puddings and their variations (my mother had numerous styles, flavours and combinations) were served. Of course, with every new concoction of steamed pudding came more beaters to lick. And who enjoyed the most beaters? I find my memory lets me down about here!

Grease a large steamed pudding basin and its lid. Get a sheet of paper that is large enough to cover the top of the bowl and also hang over the edge by 2 to 3 cm (1 in) all round. Fold a crease through its centre: this will let the paper expand as the pudding expands while cooking.

In a bowl, cream the butter and sugar until light and fluffy. Add the eggs one at a time, beating well after each addition. Add the flour and baking powder. Add the milk and mix until a smooth batter is produced. (This mixture is perhaps quicker and more successful if made in a large food processor.)

Pour the mixture into the prepared pudding basin, place the sheet of creased paper on top of the basin and place the lid on top. Steam for 45 to 55 minutes, or until firm to the touch on top. (This mixture can also be baked in individual greased ramekins or Dariole moulds.)

Serves 8

Steamed Ginger Pudding

Where fresh ginger is available, use it. But make certain you grab the ginger and not the Jerusalem artichoke, as I did in England many years ago, in another recipe, or it will lose its punch! Should fresh ginger be unavailable, use dry crushed ginger.

Place the Grand Marnier, orange liqueur or orange juice in a saucepan and bring to the simmer. Add the sultanas and let the mixture steep for 24 hours, covered.

Grease a 1 to 1.5 litre (32 to 48 fl oz) pudding basin.

Put a saucepan (large enough to hold the pudding basin) of water on to boil.

In a bowl, cream the butter, sugar and golden syrup until light and fluffy. Add the egg and combine well. Fold in the sifted flour, bicarbonate of soda, ginger, sultanas and milk.

Pour the mixture into the greased pudding basin. Cover the top of the pudding bowl with a sheet of greaseproof paper, then a sheet of aluminium foil. Make sure both have a crease in them so that they can expand as the pudding expands.

Place the basin in the saucepan of boiling water and cook for 2 to 2½ hours. Keep the saucepan topped up with water to halfway up the sides of the basin.

Serve with warmed golden syrup and cream, or with Vanilla Anglaise (see page 117).

Serves 6 to 8

½ cup (125 ml/4 fl oz) Grand Marnier, or orange liqueur, or orange juice

½ cup (90 g/3 oz) sultanas (golden raisins)

125 g (4 oz) unsalted butter

½ cup (125 g/4 oz) sugar

2 tablespoons golden syrup (treacle)

1 egg, lightly beaten

1¼ cups (155 g/5 oz) plain (all-purpose) flour, sifted

1 teaspoon bicarbonate of soda (baking soda)

1 teaspoon ground ginger

3 tablespoons milk

Self-saucing Chocolate Pudding

This dessert is from my childhood — I could never work out how my mother made the sauce go to the bottom of the pudding while it cooked!

125 g (4 oz) unsalted butter

1 cup (250 g/8 oz) sugar

2 eggs, beaten

2 cups (250 g/8 oz) plain (all-purpose) flour, sifted

2 teaspoons baking powder

3 teaspoons cocoa powder

zest and juice of 1 orange

1 cup (250 ml/8 fl oz) milk

Sauce

1 cup (185 g/6 oz) firmly packed brown sugar

2 tablespoons cocoa powder

3 cups (750 ml/24 fl oz) boiling water

⅓ cup (90 ml/3 fl oz) Grand Marnier

Preheat the oven to 180°C (350°F). Grease a large ramekin.

In a bowl, cream the butter and sugar until light and fluffy. Add the eggs, one at a time, beating well after each addition. Add the sifted flour, baking powder, cocoa powder, orange juice and zest, and milk. Mix until the batter is smooth.

Spread the batter in the greased ramekin.

Sauce

Combine the brown sugar and cocoa powder and sprinkle this over the batter.

Combine the Grand Marnier with the boiling water, then pour this mixture over the top of the pudding.

Bake for 40 to 45 minutes.

Serve immediately.

Serves 6 to 8

Warm Orange and Almond Pudding

This sweet concoction can be served warm on cool, wintry evenings, or, if allowed to cool, with a hot sauce for lunch in autumn, or with fresh fruits during summer.

The flavours can be changed by adding dried fruits, but, for those with simple tastes, serve the dessert just as the recipe says.

Preheat the oven to 180°C (350°F). Line a 28 x 30 x 2 cm (11 x 12 x 1 in) baking tray (sheet) with butter and put baking paper (parchment) on its base.

In a bowl, cream the butter and sugar until light and fluffy. Add the eggs, one at a time, beating well after each addition. Add the golden syrup, orange zest and juice and vanilla essence. Add the sifted flour, baking powder and ground almonds and combine well.

Fill the baking tray three-quarters full, then bake for 40 to 45 minutes. Let the pudding cool slightly, then unmould it onto a moist, lightly sugar-coated tea towel. Cut out pudding discs with a 5 to 6 cm (2 in) round cutter.

Serve with Citrus Sauce (see page 115), orange zest and berries.

Serves 6 to 8

125 g (4 oz) unsalted butter, softened

⅓ cup (90 g/3 oz) sugar

2 eggs

1 level teaspoon golden syrup (treacle)

juice and finely grated zest of 2 oranges

1 teaspoon vanilla essence

¾ cup (90 g/3 oz) plain (all-purpose) flour, sifted

2 level teaspoons baking powder

¾ cup (90 g/3 oz) ground (minced) almonds

Warm Orange and Almond Pudding

College Pudding

*This is another traditional pudding recipe from England which can be used
as a basis for many variations.*

*5 tablespoons
raspberry jam (jelly)*

1 tablespoon water

125 g (4 oz) unsalted butter

½ cup (125 g/4 oz) sugar

1 egg

zest of 1 lemon

*1¼ cups (155 g/5 oz)
plain (all-purpose) flour, sifted*

1 teaspoon baking powder

½ cup (125 ml/4 fl oz) milk

Grease a large pudding basin or 6 individual Dariole moulds or ramekins.

Mix the jam with the water, then spread the mixture over the base of the pudding basin or individual moulds.

In a bowl, cream the butter and sugar until light and fluffy. Add the egg and the lemon zest and mix thoroughly. Add the sifted flour, baking powder and milk and mix to a smooth batter.

Pour the batter into the pudding basin or individual moulds and cover the top/s with a lid, baking paper (parchment) or aluminium foil.

Place the pudding/s in a steamer or saucepan of boiling water: the water should come halfway up the sides of the moulds if a saucepan is being used. Steam a whole pudding for 1½ to 2 hours, individual serves for 1 hour.

Serve immediately with Custard (see page 118), Vanilla Anglaise (see page 117) or double (whipping) cream.

Serves 6

Variations

Chocolate

Take out 2 tablespoons of flour and add 1 tablespoon of cocoa powder instead. Flavour with vanilla. Leave out the jam and serve with a rich Chocolate Sauce (see page 114).

Rainbow

Divide the mixture into 3 equal amounts. Colour one of the quantities pink using cochineal or food colouring, colour another using cocoa powder mixed with a little water, and leave the last portion plain.

Alternate the colours as you pour the mixtures into the pudding basin or moulds/ramekins.

Coconut

Add 2 tablespoons of long (shredded) coconut, the juice of 1 extra lemon and 1 extra tablespoon of milk to the mixture. Replace the jam with marmalade and serve with Citrus Sauce (see page 115).

Tarte Tatin

This delectable treat of caramelised apples covered with pastry and inverted when baked, originated in French kitchens in the early 1900s, and is renowned around the world. The dessert was invented by Madame Tatin purely as a way to use up her leftover pastry. It is so famous in its original version that few ever dare to risk criticism by changing a perfect thing!

However, I like to dare original recipes — this version is a favourite from my time in Queensland, Australia, when I was just a boy. During summer the mangoes would tease me to cook them as I viewed them from the kitchen window.

The trick is to not overcook the mangoes before the pastry is crisp. If you do, the fruit becomes a pulpy mass and may not look appealing when you serve it. However, the luscious mouth watering flavour will still remain. Use only fresh mangoes, just on the unripe side.

4–5 whole mangoes

30 g (1 oz) walnut halves

60 g (2 oz) unsalted butter

⅓ cup (60 g/2 oz) caster (superfine) sugar

225 g (7 oz) puff pastry

Preheat the oven to 180°C (350°F).

Slice the two sides of each mango from the seed and carefully peel.

Melt the butter in a heavy-based pan, 5 to 7 cm (2 to 3 in) deep and 20 to 25 cm (8 to 10 in) in diameter. Make sure there is enough butter to form a 2 to 3 mm (⅛ in) layer.

Sprinkle the sugar over the butter until it is totally absorbed. Sprinkle the chopped walnuts over the butter and sugar mixture. Place the mango halves in the pan, wide end down, as upright and close together as possible. Over low heat, cook the mangoes for 12 to 15 minutes.

On a lightly floured surface, roll the pastry out to the size of the pan's diameter. Prick it heavily with a fork or docker.

Cover the mango with the pastry, tucking it in at the edges.

Place the dish in the oven and bake for 30 to 40 minutes. Remove the Tarte Tatin from the oven and let it rest for several minutes. Turn out onto a platter, upside down, and serve warm or cold with cream.

Serves 6

Lemon Possit

I am often asked what my favourite dessert is, and it would have to be this simple, yet extraordinarily smooth and velvety lemon cream — maybe because it contains so few ingredients but still can really test any cook.

Your first attempt at this dessert may not be terrifically successful, but do not be deterred. The trick is to boil the mixture until it has reduced enough to set upon cooling. A rich, sweet yet tart cream will be the reward for those who persevere.

3 cups (750 ml/24 fl oz) double (whipping) cream

1¼ cups (310 g/10 oz) sugar

juice of 3 lemons

6 champagne flutes

Place all ingredients in a very large saucepan, and mix lightly together.

Bring the mixture to the boil. When it has reached a rapid boil, reduce the heat slightly so that it is gently boiling (not just simmering). Boil the mixture for 30 minutes, skimming the surface to remove any frothy residue.

Remove from the heat and cool slightly before ladling into the champagne flutes. Refrigerate the mixtures for 4 hours (or overnight), until they are chilled and firm.

Pour a thin layer of single (light) cream over the top of each Possit and serve.

Serves 6

Muscat Pears

juice of 2 lemons

10 cups (2.5 litres/5 pints) water

6–8 large, firm, ripe pears

1⅓ cups (310 g/10 oz) sugar

1 cup (250 ml/8 fl oz) muscat

juice and zest of 2 oranges

Pears are one of the few fruits which I truly adore, eat regularly away from my work, and actively seek out to cook with. This simple combination of muscat syrup and pears is an easy recipe and one which can be experimented with, though part of its beauty is the colour that the muscat gives to the outside of the pears. You can use different muscats and even different alcoholic bases for the poaching syrup. This summer dessert is very refreshing after a light meal. With a good quality muscat, these pears should taste absolutely superb.

Mix the lemon juice with 8 cups (2 litres/4 pints) of water. Peel the pears and dip them in the acidulated water so that they do not brown or discolour.

In a large saucepan, place 2 cups (500 ml/16 fl oz) of water, the sugar and muscat and the juice and zest of the oranges. Bring the mixture to the boil.

Immerse the pears carefully in the boiling syrup and place an undersized lid on the saucepan to keep the pears submerged during cooking. Simmer the mixture for 30 minutes, or until the pears are soft when pierced with a knife.

Remove the pears with a slotted spoon and place them on a large serving platter or plate with the remaining syrup.

Serve the pears with a small amount of their own syrup.

Serves 6 to 8

Muscat Pears

Clafoutis

2 cups (500 ml/16 fl oz) milk

1 cup (250 ml/8 fl oz)
single (light) cream

¾ cup (90 g/3 oz)
plain (all-purpose) flour, sifted

1¼ cups (225 g/7 oz)
icing (powdered) sugar, sifted

4 eggs

310 g (10 oz) chopped fresh
fruits, such as peaches,
plums, or berries

icing (powdered) sugar,
for dusting

During my apprenticeship I worked at a restaurant that served this French traditional dessert on its daily lunchtime buffet, where it proved to be one of the most popular desserts. I saved the recipe but did not use it for many years as I did not particularly like it. However, I recently experienced the clafoutis again in Paris and fell in love immediately.

Much of the dessert's success depends on which fruit is placed at the bottom of the batter. Plums and sour black cherries are among the more traditional and most flavoursome, but fresh peach and apricot make for a taste sensation as well.

Preheat the oven to 180°C (350°F).

Place the cream and milk in a saucepan and bring to the boil.

In a bowl, whisk the flour, sifted icing sugar and eggs until combined.

Remove the boiling liquid from the heat and pour it over the mixture, whisking continuously. Whisk until the mixture forms a smooth batter, then continue until the batter cools.

Let the mixture rest in the refrigerator for 1 hour.

Place the chopped fresh fruits in the base of a large buttered ramekin or pie dish and pour the batter over.

Bake for 35 to 45 minutes, or until the top is golden brown and the clafoutis is set firm.

Dust heavily with icing sugar and serve immediately.

Serves 6

Rhubarb Crumble

This is one of the easiest and most versatile of pudding recipes, because it does not matter what fruit is used, as long as there is plenty of crumble on top.

Crumble recipes also vary, from the simple and easy (as here) to the highly flavoured (containing muesli, coconut, nuts and other ingredients). I like this recipe because it is quick and easy, perfect for those who do not wish to spend ages in the kitchen.

Since early childhood I have loved crumbles (called streusel and Brown Betty in other countries). Perhaps the strongest memory I have regarding crumbles is from when my sister had first left home to get married. I was staying with her for several days, and she was attempting to impress the family's apprentice chef. When it came time for dessert, she told me of a new recipe which was a flavour combination success and was also healthy for me.

At that age I was always inconsiderate of others' feelings, and at the time I was absolutely starving. So when my sister served her masterpiece of a crumble and it was the size of a 20 cent piece (dime) I could do nothing but laugh — of course this was healthy, there wasn't even enough to stick to the sides of my stomach!

My laughter resulted in tears and hysterics and my poor sister has never attempted another crumble — for me, at least. I dedicate this recipe to her, and hope that one day she might again brave the wrath of her brother and cook it for me.

¾ cup (185 g/6 oz) sugar

60 g (2 oz) unsalted butter

¾ cup (185 ml/6 fl oz) water

6 apples, peeled, cored and chopped into small pieces

zest of 2 lemons

zest of 1 orange

Crumble Topping

1 cup (125 g/4 oz) plain (all-purpose) flour

2 teaspoons ground cinnamon

½ cup (125 g/4 oz) sugar

100 g (3½ oz) unsalted butter

icing (powdered) sugar, for dusting

Preheat the oven to 180°C (350°F).

In a saucepan, place the sugar, butter and water. Heat until the sugar and butter dissolve, and you have a syrup. Bring the syrup to the boil, then add the apple and lemon and orange zest. Cover and simmer for 5 minutes, or until the apple is tender but not mushy. Let the mixture cool in a stainless steel bowl.

Spoon the mixture into ramekins.

Crumble Topping

Place the flour, cinnamon and sugar in a bowl and rub the butter through until the mixture resembles fresh breadcrumbs.

Sprinkle the top of each ramekin with the crumble mixture. Bake for 15 to 20 minutes, or until the crumble is golden brown on top.

Dust lightly with icing sugar and serve.

Serves 6

Apple Fritters

There is nothing more delicious than a fresh fritter cooked in a crisp beer batter, covered with a sweet dusting of icing sugar and served with a tart cranberry or raspberry coulis. I like this recipe because any type of fruit can be dipped into the easy-to-prepare beer batter. Bananas, apples, plums, cherries and most other fruits make delicious fritters. Just remember that fruits with a high water content, such as oranges and strawberries, do not make good fritters as they boil away to nothing during frying.

60 g (2 oz) fresh compressed yeast

2 cups (500 ml/16 fl oz) beer

1½ teaspoons salt

3 cups (375 g/12 oz) plain (all-purpose) flour

3 apples, peeled and cored

1¼ cups (155 g/5 oz) plain (all-purpose) flour, extra

deep fryer or deep frypan of oil, heated

icing (powdered) sugar, for dusting

In a bowl, lightly whisk the yeast in the beer to dissolve it. Add the flour and the salt and stir to a thick paste. Place the bowl in a warm area for 2 hours to ferment. The mixture should double in bulk.

Slice the apples into 2 cm (¾ in) thick slices. Coat both sides of the slices lightly with the extra flour, then dip them quickly into the yeast batter. Make sure each apple slice is completely coated.

Carefully place the apple slices in the heated cooking oil (180°C/350°F) and cook until both sides are golden brown. Remove from the oil, dust lightly with icing sugar, and serve with fruit and cream.

Serves 6

Apple Fritters

Jam Roly Poly

2½ cups (310 g/10 oz)
plain (all-purpose) flour, sifted

3 teaspoons baking powder

185 g (6 oz) shredded suet

1¼–1½ cups (310–375 ml/
10–12 fl oz) cold water

310 g (10 oz) plum jam (jelly)

This heavy dough makes an unconventional pudding that is famous throughout the United Kingdom; perhaps because it is so simple to make, or perhaps because it is so rich and sinful and exactly what one needs during the depths of a chilly winter.

The pudding can be boiled or baked. The richer the flavour of the jam, the better.

I think the main reason this dessert holds a place amongst my favourites is that it is a comfort food. When we are so used to being told everything is bad for us and that we are all too heavy or not exercising the right way, I know that when I am curled up in front of the fire and eating this comforting dessert, I won't care about any of that!

Preheat the oven to 200°C (400°F). Lightly grease a 28 x 30 x 3 cm (11 x 12 x 1 in) baking tray (sheet).

In a bowl, mix the sifted flour, baking powder and shredded suet with the water, to make a firm dough. Let the dough rest for 5 minutes. Roll out the dough on a lightly floured bench (counter top) to 25 x 30 cm (10 x 12 in) and spread it with the jam.

Roll the roly poly up like a Swiss roll, rolling from the furthest edge slowly and tightly towards yourself.

Bake for 35 to 45 minutes.

Serve immediately with Sweet White Sauce (see page 118) or Custard (see page 118).

Serves 4 to 5

Baked Apples

*A stunningly simple pudding for winter or summer. You can change the central
filling of these delights as often, and in as many ways, as you like.*

*Living in the state of Australia known as the 'Apple Isle' (Tasmania), my mother
would make these during apple season each year and serve them piping hot from the
oven with fresh custard. To this day, serving this dessert evokes
memories of childhood.*

*In France the apples are peeled, filled, covered in a large square of puff pastry and
eaten as a dessert or large snack.*

6 apples, cored

¾ cup (100 g/3½ oz)
ground (meal) almonds

1 tablespoon
golden syrup (treacle)

¼ cup (90 ml/3 fl oz) honey

½ cup (60 g/2 oz) currants

⅓ cup (60 g/2 oz) brown sugar

zest of 1 orange

60 g (2 oz) unsalted butter

Preheat the oven to 180°C (350°F).

Place the cored apples in a deep baking dish.

In a bowl, mix the almonds, syrup, honey, currants, sugar and orange zest.
Spoon the filling mixture into the centre of the apples and pack it in firmly. Use
up all the mixture. Top each apple with a teaspoon of butter.

Bake the apples for 35 to 40 minutes, or until they are soft when pierced with
a knife or skewer.

Serve immediately, with Custard (see page 118).

Serves 6

Sago Plum Pudding

⅓ cup (60 g/2 oz) sago

1 cup (250 ml/8 fl oz) milk

½ cup (90 g/3 oz)
sultanas (golden raisins)

1 tablespoon brandy

1½ cups (90 g/3 oz)
fresh breadcrumbs

1 teaspoon cinnamon

½ cup (125 g/4 oz) sugar

6 teaspoons unsalted butter,
melted

1 teaspoon bicarbonate of soda
(baking soda)

*Sago is not often used these days, but it is a surprisingly simple ingredient to use and
makes a tasty dessert. When I was first asked to make this dish in England I did not
want to reveal that I had never heard of it, let alone made it. A quick phone call to my
mum produced this dish, and I have now been serving it for nearly a decade.
Many of my customers enjoy it and have even requested its return when
I have tired of it and removed it from my menu.*

Soak the sago in the milk for 2 to 3 hours (or overnight) in the refrigerator.

Soak the sultanas in the brandy overnight.

Grease a 1 to 1.5 litre (32 to 48 fl oz) pudding bowl and lid.

In a bowl, combine the breadcrumbs, cinnamon, sugar and brandy-soaked
sultanas. Mix in the soaked sago (and any milk which remains). Mix the melted
butter and bicarbonate of soda, then combine this with the mixture.

Place the batter in the greased pudding bowl and cover with the lid.

Steam the pudding for 1½ to 2 hours, then serve immediately with Custard
(see page 118) or Vanilla Anglaise (see page 117).

Serves 6

PASTRIES

This is truly a chapter with recipes for everybody and for every occasion, from the formal High Tea to a casual afternoon snack.

Indulge yourself in anything from a traditional fruit cake to a light and luscious Strawberry Delice.

Pineapple and Carrot Muffins

I love the idea of fresh muffins, piping hot and dripping with butter and jam, every day, for breakfast or for morning snacks. These muffins are almost a healthy treat — they are moist and delicious and will have your family and friends returning time and time again.

Life has many pleasures and these are among them!

1¼ cups (155 g/5 oz) plain (all-purpose) flour

1 cup (125 g/4 oz) wholemeal flour

⅓ cup (60 g/2 oz) brown sugar

1 teaspoon baking powder

1 teaspoon bicarbonate soda (baking soda)

1 teaspoon cinnamon

¾ cup (125 g/4 oz) grated carrot

1 cup (250 g/8 oz) drained crushed pineapple

1 cup (185 ml/6 fl oz) plain yoghurt

2 egg whites

4 tablespoons vegetable oil

Preheat the oven to 180°C (350°F).

Lightly grease a 12-cup large muffin tray or 24-cup small muffin tray.

In a large bowl mix together the flours, brown sugar, baking powder, bicarbonate of soda and cinnamon.

In another bowl stir together the carrots, pineapple, yoghurt, egg whites and oil, mixing enough to break up the egg whites.

Make a well in the centre of the flour and add the wet mixture. Mix together lightly, only until all ingredients are combined.

Spread the batter into the greased muffin cups and bake for 15 to 20 minutes, or until firm to the touch.

Cool the muffins in their pan for several minutes before removing them.

Makes 12 large or 24 small muffins

Previous page: Lemon Meringue Tarts, page 104

Plain Scones

Whilst living and working in England, I came to love the institution of Afternoon or High Tea, especially at places like the Ritz Hotel, where the scones are feathery light and very moreish with their fresh jam and clotted cream.

In some countries scones are known as biscuits and are served with savoury foods such as soups and fried meals. If this is what you want to make, just leave out the sugar and cinnamon, and you will have a savoury-style scone or biscuit for any occasion.

2¼ cups (280 g/9 oz) plain (all-purpose) flour

½ teaspoon cinnamon

1½ teaspoons baking powder (baking soda)

1 teaspoon salt

3 teaspoons sugar

60 g (2 oz) unsalted butter

¾ cup (185 ml/6 fl oz) milk

Preheat the oven to 260°C (500°F) and grease and flour a scone tray.

Sift the flour, cinnamon, baking powder and salt into a large bowl, then stir in the sugar.

Chop the butter into small pieces and rub it into the sifted ingredients, until the mixture has the consistency of breadcrumbs.

Make a well in the centre of the mixture and pour in the milk.

Using a knife, stir and cut the mixture until it forms a soft dough.

Place the dough on a lightly floured surface and knead it lightly for a few seconds. Then pat the dough into a 2 to 3 cm (1 to 1¼ in) thickness.

Cut out the scones with a 4 to 5 cm (1¾ to 2 in) round cookie cutter which has been dipped into flour.

Place the scones on the baking tray. They should be touching each other.

Brush the tops of the scones with milk and leave them in a warm place for 15 minutes.

Bake in the preheated oven for 12 to 15 minutes, or until golden brown on top and base.

Place the scones on a cake rack to cool, then break them off as required.

(Note: If the scones are close to each other on the baking tray, they will push each other up during baking.)

Makes 10 to 12 scones

Orange Pecan Doughnuts

Packed full of nuts and covered with a sensational chocolate glaze, these doughnuts will be sure winners with children. Do not be too fussed if these doughnuts split as they cook; it just gives more crevices for the glaze to hide in.

This recipe was given to me by a United States chef who was on an exchange program in England during my time there as pastrychef. He gave me the recipe on the understanding that a fresh batch be made every two to three days, as he was missing home, hot dogs and doughnuts!

3½ cups (435 g/14 oz)
plain (all-purpose) flour

¾ cup (90 g/3 oz)
pecan nuts, lightly roasted

1 cup (250 g/8 oz) sugar

4 teaspoons baking powder

2 teaspoons salt

1 teaspoon ground cinnamon

1 egg

1 cup (250 ml/8 fl oz) milk

3 tablespoons vegetable oil

2 teaspoons vanilla essence

vegetable oil for frying

In a food processor fitted with a metal chopping blade, combine ½ cup (60 g/2 oz) of flour with the pecans, and process until the nuts are coarsely chopped. Place this mixture, the remaining flour, the sugar, baking powder, salt and cinnamon in a large mixing bowl.

In another bowl, whisk together the egg, milk, oil and vanilla.

Add the liquid to the dry ingredients and combine, using a wooden spoon.

Knead the dough, on a lightly floured surface, until it becomes smooth.

Place the dough between two sheets of baking paper (parchment) and roll it to 2½ to 3 cm (1 to 1¼ in) thickness. Place the flattened dough on a baking tray, cover with plastic wrap (cling film), and freeze it for 30 to 40 minutes.

Remove the dough from the freezer and take off the plastic wrap. Cut discs of pastry, using a floured 8 cm (3¼ in) round cookie cutter. Then, using a floured 3 cm (1¼ in) round cookie cutter, cut the centre out of each disc.

Place the doughnuts and holes on a lined tray, cover with plastic wrap, and refrigerate for a further 40 minutes. Remove the doughnuts from the refrigerator, take off the plastic wrap, and let them stand for 15 minutes. Heat a pan of oil or a deep fryer to 180°C (350°F) and fry the holes first (adjust the temperature of the oil if necessary).

Fry the first doughnut for about 1 minute on either side, or until golden. Let it cool slightly, then break it in half and check that it is cooked. If it is not cooked, reduce the heat of the oil a little, then cook the other doughnuts.

Cool the cooked holes and doughnuts on trays covered with paper towels (absorbent kitchen paper).

Chocolate Glaze

¾ cup (185 ml/6 fl oz) water

juice and zest of 1 orange

¼ cup (60 g/2 oz) sugar

2 tablespoons glucose

500 g (1 lb) cooking chocolate, melted

Chocolate Orange Glaze

Place the water, orange zest and juice, sugar and glucose in a saucepan and bring to a simmer. Stir until the sugar is completely dissolved. Remove from the heat and add the melted chocolate, slowly, stirring until all is combined.

Transfer the chocolate mixture to a bowl and place the bowl over a pot of simmering water. Dip the cooled doughnuts (one at a time) into the chocolate glaze so they are half-coated, then cool them on cake racks.

Serve immediately, or store. Doughnuts will keep for 2 to 3 days in an airtight container in the refrigerator.

Makes 14 to16 doughnuts and 14 to 16 holes!

Orange Pecan Doughnuts

Pecan Tartlets

5 cups (625 g/20 oz)
plain (all-purpose) flour

1½ cups (280 g/9 oz)
icing (powdered) sugar

310 g (10 oz) unsalted butter,
chopped into small pieces

1 tablespoon water

1 egg

1 egg yolk

Filling

6 eggs

½ cup (90 g /3 oz) brown sugar

2 cups (500 ml/16 fl oz)
maple syrup

½ cup (125 ml/4 fl oz)
coffee liqueur

2½ cups (310 g/10 oz)
whole pecan nuts

No matter where you travel, or when, don't be surprised if, during your gastronomic explorations, you find these rich treasures on at least one menu.

These tartlets have a crisp sweet pastry crust, filled with a soft, rich mixture of sweet syrups (which sets in the oven) and covered with pecan nuts.

They can be large or small, glazed with apricot jam, dusted with icing sugar or left plain, and can be served with cream, ice cream or on their own.

Preheat the oven to 180°C (350°F).

Place the flour, icing sugar and butter in a large mixing bowl and combine until the mixture resembles coarse breadcrumbs.

Add the water, egg and egg yolk, and mix to a dough.

Seal the dough in plastic wrap (cling film) and refrigerate it for 40 to 45 minutes.

Roll the pastry to a thickness of 2 to 3 mm (⅒ in) and line eight 10 cm (4 in) tartlet moulds (the kind with removable bases).

Line the pastry shells with baking paper (parchment) or waxed (greaseproof) paper and fill with rice or baking weights.

Bake for 10 to 12 minutes, then remove from the oven, and remove the weights and paper.

In a bowl, whisk the eggs with the brown sugar until the sugar is dissolved. Stir in the maple syrup and coffee liqueur. Pour the mixture into the pastry shells.

Arrange the pecan halves in a pattern on top.

Bake the tartlets for 25 to 30 minutes, or until the middle is completely set.

Remove the tartlets from the oven and let them cool slightly before taking them out of the moulds and serving them.

Makes 8 tartlets

Lemon Curd Tartlets

If you like small sweet treats with a little bite, then these baked curd tartlets are for you. You can make them large or small, and you can also use this sensational curd paste as a filling in cakes and other desserts.

Pastry Cases

Preheat the oven to 180°C (350°F).

Place the flour and icing sugar in a bowl with the butter. Rub the butter into the dry ingredients until the mixture resembles coarse breadcrumbs.

Add the egg yolks and work the mixture to a dough.

Wrap the dough in plastic wrap (cling film) and refrigerate it for 40 minutes.

On a lightly floured board, roll the pastry to a 2 to 3 mm (1/10 in) thickness.

Using an 8 cm (3¼ in) plain round cutter cut out 18 discs of the pastry and line individual 5 to 6 cm (2 to 2½ in) brioche or tart shells with the discs.

Place a sheet of baking paper in the base of each lined tart shell and fill the shells with rice or beads. Blind bake the shells for 10 to 12 minutes, or until the pastry is golden brown around the edges and lightly baked through on the base.

Filling

Place all the ingredients in a large mixing bowl and whisk lightly until combined.

Place the bowl over a saucepan of simmering water and let the curd mixture heat and cook, whisking continuously.

When the mixture is thick enough to coat the back of a spoon, remove the bowl from the heat and let the mixture cool. When it is cool, refrigerate the lemon curd overnight.

Fill each of the tartlet shells three-quarters full with the mixture.

Place the tartlets (still in their moulds or tins) on a baking tray and bake them for 15 to 20 minutes at 180°C (350°F).

Remove the tarts from the oven and let them cool. Unmould them from their tins and serve them dusted with icing sugar and garnished with lemon zest.

Makes 18 tartlets

Pastry Cases

2 cups (250 g/8 oz)
plain (all-purpose) flour, sifted

¼ cup (75 g/2½ oz)
icing (powdered) sugar

155 g (5 oz) unsalted butter,
chopped into 1 cm (½ in) cubes

2 egg yolks

Filling

zest and juice of 5 lemons

5 eggs

4 egg yolks

¾ cup (185 g/6 oz) sugar

2 tablespoons milk

200 g (6½ oz) unsalted butter

lemon zest, to garnish

icing (powdered) sugar,
for dusting

Engadiners

These Swiss tartlets (or one single tart) contain sweet, rich, creamy caramel, which enrobes the nuts of your choice, all enclosed in a sweet pastry case.

Be careful when making the caramel — sugar burns are nasty. If you use a long-handled spoon you shouldn't have any problems. These delights are extremely rich, so make them small — they can then be enjoyed rather than laboured over!

Pastry Cases

Pastry Cases

2 cups (250 g/8 oz) plain (all-purpose) flour, sifted

75 g (2½ oz) icing (powdered) sugar

155 g (5 oz) unsalted butter, chopped into 1 cm (½ in) cubes

2 egg yolks

125 g (4 oz) dark (plain or semi-sweet) chocolate, melted

Preheat the oven to 180°C (350°F).

Place the flour and icing sugar in a bowl.

Rub the butter into the flour and sugar until the mixture resembles coarse breadcrumbs.

Add the egg yolks and work the mixture to a dough.

Seal the dough in plastic wrap (cling film) and refrigerate it for 40 minutes.

On a lightly floured board, roll the pastry to a 2 to 3 mm (⅒ in) thickness.

Using an 8 cm (3¼ in) plain round cutter, cut out discs of pastry and line 8 to 10 brioche or tart shells (5 to 6 cm/2 to 2¼ in) with the discs.

Place a sheet of baking paper (parchment) in the base of each lined tart shell, then fill the shells with rice or baking weights and blind bake them for 10 to 12 minutes, or until the pastry is golden brown around the edges and the base is lightly baked through.

Let the pastry shells cool, then brush the inside of each one with the melted chocolate.

Caramel

Caramel

⅔ cup (155 g/5 oz) sugar

1 tablespoon honey

½ cup (125 ml/4 fl oz) single (light) cream

60 g (2 oz) unsalted butter

1¼ cups (155 g/5 oz) finely chopped walnuts

dark (plain or semi-sweet) chocolate curls, for decoration

Place a large saucepan over the heat and heat slowly. Sprinkle in a small amount of the sugar and let it melt. Slowly add a little more sugar. Make sure the sugar remains golden brown.

Add the honey, cream and butter, and stir. Use a long-handled wooden spoon so that your hands and fingers are not scalded by steam from the pan. Stir continuously to make sure no lumps of sugar remain.

Add the chopped walnuts and stir well.

Let the mixture cool slightly, then pour it into the chocolate-lined pastry cases. Refrigerate the engadiners overnight.

Serve with double (whipping) cream, topped with dark Chocolate Curls (see page 123).

Makes 8 to 10 tarts

Lemon Curd Tartlets, page 89, and Engadiners

Swiss Roll

*1 cup (125 g/4 oz)
plain (all-purpose) flour*

½ teaspoon cinnamon

½ teaspoon ground cloves

*1 cup (225 g/7 oz)
caster (superfine) sugar*

8 egg yolks

*⅔ cup (125 g/4 oz)
icing (powdered) sugar,
plus extra, for dusting*

8 egg whites

*⅔ cup (250 g/8 oz)
raspberry jam, warmed*

The thicker (but not richer) cousin of the roulade, the Swiss roll has graced the dessert trolleys of English High Teas for centuries. Because Swiss rolls are not too rich, they tend to disappear very quickly, even when it is not afternoon tea time!

This Swiss roll recipe combines marzipan and a rich almond flavour in the sponge base, which remains moist and luscious for days. Easy to make, easy to bake and delicious to eat, I hope this recipe helps the Swiss roll remain a classic in the pastry department for a long time to come.

Preheat oven to 200°C (400°F). Grease a 23 x 20 x 1 cm (9 x 8 x ½ in) Swiss roll pan very lightly with butter and line with baking paper (parchment).

Sift the flour, cinnamon and cloves twice. Sprinkle a large sheet of greaseproof paper with the caster sugar.

In a bowl, beat the egg yolks with the icing sugar until the mixture becomes thick and fluffy and pale in colour.

In another bowl, beat the egg whites until they form stiff peaks.

Fold the egg whites into the egg yolk mixture, then slowly and carefully fold in the sifted flour and spices.

Spread the mixture evenly into the prepared tray and bake for 20 to 25 minutes, or until it is golden brown and springs back when touched.

Turn the sponge out onto the sugared greaseproof paper and trim the crusty edges. It is important to work quickly at this stage. Spread the sponge with jam. Then, starting with a short side, roll the sponge tightly towards you. Place the roll, seam down, on the greaseproof paper and roll the greaseproof paper around the Swiss roll. Using a scraper, tighten the roll.

Dust with icing sugar and serve in thin slices.

Chocolate Peanut Roulade

Many people ask about the difference between a roulade and a Swiss roll.
They look similar, but a roulade is a thinner cake and is turned or rolled many
times, while a Swiss roll is made of thicker sponge, always contains jam and
has a maximum of three rolls or turns.
This sweet roulade is fit for a prize banquet and is not so hard to produce.

Buttercream

Place the sugar, golden syrup and water in a saucepan and bring to the boil. Place the egg whites in a mixing bowl.

Boil the sugar mixture steadily, stirring occasionally, till the mixture reaches 118°C (240°F) — soft ball stage. This will take 2 to 4 minutes.

While the sugar syrup is boiling, begin whipping the egg whites. Continue until they are holding stiff peaks.

Slowly drizzle the sugar syrup into the egg whites. Continue whisking at high speed until the syrup is incorporated and the meringue is beginning to cool.

In another bowl, whip the butter until it is light and soft and pale.

Add the meringue to the butter in small amounts, whisking together well. When all the meringue has been incorporated, add the chopped peanut pieces.

Sponge Base

Preheat the oven to 180°C (350°F). Line a 40 x 35 cm (16 x 14 in) baking tray with baking paper (parchment).

Dissolve the instant coffee in the water, then blend this into the egg yolks. Mix the melted chocolate into the egg yolk mixture.

In another bowl, beat the egg whites until they hold stiff peaks. Drizzle the sugar in slowly, down the side of the mixer, while the machine is still whisking. Keep whisking until the sugar is dissolved.

Fold the chocolate mixture into the egg whites, then spread the mixture quickly onto the lined tray. Bake for 12 to 15 minutes, or until the cake springs back when touched in the centre.

Place a sheet of greaseproof paper, lightly dusted with cocoa, on top of a moist towel. Invert the baked cake onto this paper. Carefully peel away the baking paper the cake was baked on, then quickly roll up the cake from the shortest edge, making sure the cocoa-dusted paper rolls up with it. Let the cake cool on a cake rack, then carefully unroll it.

Spread the cake with the buttercream, then re-roll it into a tight cylinder. Use the towel to help get a firm roll. Place the cake straight in the freezer and leave it there for 1 to 2 hours. Then store it, covered, in the refrigerator until required. The cake will keep for 1 to 2 days.

Buttercream

⅓ cup (90 g/3 oz) sugar

½ cup (185 ml/6 fl oz) golden syrup (treacle)

90 ml (3 fl oz) water

3 egg whites

250 g (8 oz) unsalted butter

90 g (3 oz) chopped peanuts

Flourless Sponge

3 level tablespoons instant coffee granules

¼ cup (60 ml/2 fl oz) water

6 eggs, separated

185 g (6 oz) dark (plain or semi-sweet) chocolate, melted

½ cup (125 g/4 oz) sugar

Ganache

¾ cup (185 ml/6 fl oz) single (light) cream

310 g (10 oz) dark (plain or semi-sweet) chocolate, finely chopped

60 g (2 oz) unsalted butter, softened

finely grated zest of 1 orange

30 ml (1 fl oz) orange liqueur

lightly roasted unsalted peanuts, finely crushed

icing (powdered) sugar, for dusting

Ganache

Place the cream in a saucepan and bring to the boil. Remove the cream from the heat, add the chocolate and let the mixture stand for 2 to 3 minutes; stir it to a thick paste.

Let the mixture cool slightly, then whisk in the softened butter, orange zest and liqueur. Refrigerate the ganache until it is a spreading consistency (about 30 minutes).

Assembling the Roulade

Spread the sides and top of the rolled-up cake with the ganache. Press the finely crushed peanuts into the ganache and refrigerate the roulade for a further hour. Lightly dust with icing sugar before serving.

Serves 12 to 16

Citrus Tantalisers

125g (4 oz) unsalted butter

½ cup (90 g/3 oz) icing (powdered) sugar

1¼ cups (155 g/5 oz) plain (all-purpose) flour

Topping

2 eggs

zest and juice of 1 lemon

zest and juice of 1 orange

¼ cup (30 g/1 oz) plain (all-purpose) flour

1¼ cups (250 g/8 oz) caster (superfine) sugar

icing (powdered) sugar, for dusting

Preheat the oven to 160°C (320°F)

Grease and line an 18 x 28 x 2 cm (7 x 11 x 1 in) baking tray (sheet) with baking paper (parchment).

In a bowl, mix the butter, icing sugar and flour in a bowl until smooth and soft in texture. Press the mixture evenly and smoothly into the base of the prepared tray and bake in the preheated oven for 15 minutes, or until just beginning to brown.

Remove and allow to cool in tray. Maintain the oven temperature.

Pour the topping over the prepared base and return to the oven for a further 20 minutes.

Remove and immediately dust heavily with icing sugar. Allow to cool in the tray for 2 hours before cutting into slices.

Topping

Lightly whisk the eggs. Add the lemon and orange zest and juice and whisk to combine.

In a separate bowl, mix the flour and sugar, then whisk in the egg mixture. Continue whisking until the mixture is smooth.

Makes 24 slices

Chocolate Peanut Roulade

Apple Strudel

Austria is famous for strudel served with lashings of sweetened cream or Crème Anglaise.

I always respected the Austrians for having produced the strudel but I then met Hungarians who strongly protested against the idea that Austria invented strudel dough. In fact, they are correct; the Hungarians were the first to use strudel dough — they were trying to copy the phyllo pastry of the Middle East!

The trick to a good strudel is the thinness of the pastry. The filling is really almost secondary. It can be any flavour you like, so use the apple filling given here, or produce your own unique dessert.

Dough

310 g (10 oz) plain (all-purpose) flour or strong (bread) flour

⅛ teaspoon salt

1 egg

¾ cup (185 m/6 fl oz) water

1 tablespoon vegetable oil

Filling

250 g (8 oz) melted butter

1½ cups (90 g/3 oz) fresh breadcrumbs

1 teaspoon cinnamon

finely grated zest of 1 orange

½ cup (90 g/3 oz) sultanas

60 g (2 oz) unsalted butter, melted, extra

⅔ cup (155 g/5 oz) sugar

5 fresh cooking apples, peeled, cored and finely sliced

Preheat the oven to 180°C (350°F).

Sift the flour and salt into a bowl.

In another bowl, beat the egg, then beat in the water and oil. Using first a knife and then one hand, mix the water and egg mixture into the flour, making a soft dough. Add more water if necessary. Knead the dough until it is smooth and elastic.

Place the dough in a clean, lightly floured dish, cover, and leave in a warm place for 15 to 20 minutes.

While the dough rests, heat the melted butter in a frypan. When it is hot, quickly fry the breadcrumbs until they are golden brown. Place them in a bowl and fold through the cinnamon, orange zest and sultanas.

Place the dough on a large floured tablecloth or sheet. Beginning from an edge, pull and stretch the dough slowly. As the edge becomes thinner, start the process again from the centre. Use the back of your hands to lift, pull and stretch the dough slowly, until it becomes paper-thin all over.

When the dough is paper-thin, brush it thoroughly with the extra melted unsalted butter, reserving a little.

Sprinkle the buttered dough with the breadcrumb mixture, the sugar and the sliced apples.

Fold the sides of the pastry in, towards the centre. Use the cloth or sheet to help roll up the strudel tightly. Tip the strudel from the cloth onto a baking tray and coat it with the reserved melted butter.

Bake in the preheated oven for 30 to 35 minutes, then serve immediately, dusted with icing sugar.

Serves 6 to 8

Chelsea Bun

All good afternoon teas should contain one bread line, such as a sweet loaf. Chelsea buns are a favourite and can be served sliced or whole (so everybody can break their own piece from the big loaf).

You can make this recipe your own by adding different fruits and nuts and flavourings before rolling the bun and cutting it.

2 cups (250 g/8 oz) plain (all-purpose) flour

30 g (1 oz) sugar

60 g (2 oz) unsalted butter

15 g (½ oz) fresh (compressed) yeast

1 egg

water

60 g (2 oz) currants

30 g (1 oz) mixed (candied) peel

30 g (1 oz) brown sugar

½ teaspoon cinnamon

icing (powdered) sugar, for dusting

Place the flour and sugar in a mixing bowl and mix. Cut in the butter and yeast and mix until the mixture resembles fresh bread crumbs.

Make a well in the centre of the mixture and add the egg and a little water. Form the mixture into a dough. Knead the dough for 5 to 8 minutes, until it is smooth and elastic, then let it rest for 30 to 40 minutes, or until it is double its original size.

Punch down the dough and on a lightly floured surface roll it to a 30 x 30 cm (12 x 12 in) square.

Brush the top of the dough with milk and sprinkle over the currants, mixed peel, sugar and cinnamon.

Starting with the side furthest from you, roll the dough tightly towards you, as if it were a Swiss roll. When the dough is completely rolled, cut it into seven equal portions.

Line a 20 cm (8 in) round buttered tin with baking (parchment) paper. Place 6 of the cut buns around the edge, cut side up, and place the last one in the centre, again with the cut side up.

Preheat the oven to 180°C (350°F).

Place the tin in a warm area for 40 to 45 minutes, until the buns have doubled in size.

Bake the buns in the preheated oven for 35 to 40 minutes, or until they are golden brown.

Place a cake rack over the top of the buns and invert the tin to turn the buns out. Dust the tops of the buns lightly with icing sugar and serve immediately.

Serves 7

Apple Tea Cake

*Afternoon and morning teas are usually (but not in England!) just a short break
from work, a time when a quick drink and a light snack will do.
At these times, when a major dessert, cake or pastry is not required,
Apple Tea Cake can come in handy. Serve it in thin slices
(you can spread them with butter, too) for a quick pick-me-up
at the beginning or the end of the day.*

Preheat the oven to 180°C (350°F). Grease a 20 cm (8 in) sponge cake tin.

Sift together the flour, baking powder, nutmeg, cinnamon and cocoa.

Cream the butter and sugar until light and fluffy.

Mix the bicarbonate of soda into the apple and beat this into the creamed
butter and sugar.

Stir in the flour and spices, and the sultanas, then add the milk. Stir until
combined.

Pour the mixture into the sponge cake tin and bake it in the preheated oven
for 40 to 45 minutes.

Turn the cake onto a wire rack to cool. When it is cold, ice the cake with
White Butter Icing (see page 123) and sprinkle it lightly with cinnamon.

Serves 10 to 14

1¼ cups (155 g/5 oz)
plain (all-purpose) flour

2 teaspoons baking powder
(baking soda)

1 teaspoon nutmeg

1 teaspoon cinnamon

1 tablespoon cocoa

60 g (2 oz) unsalted butter

5 tablespoons sugar

1 teaspoon bicarbonate of soda

1 cup (250 g/8 oz) hot stewed
apple, not too moist

¾ cup (125 g/4 oz) sultanas
(golden raisins)

¾ cup (185 ml/6 fl oz) milk

cinnamon, for dusting

Apple Tea Cake

High Tea Fruit Cake

2½ cups (310 g/10 oz)
plain (all-purpose) flour

2½ teaspoons baking powder

2 teaspoons ground cinnamon

1 level teaspoon ground cloves

250 g (8 oz) unsalted butter

1 cup (250 g/8 oz) sugar

3 tablespoons marmalade

4 eggs

½ cup (90 g/3 oz)
sultanas (golden raisins)

⅓ cup (60 g/2 oz)
mixed (candied) peel

⅓ cup (60 g/2 oz)
seedless (dark) raisins

¾ cup (90 g/3 oz)
almonds, roughly chopped

As an apprentice pastrychef I was taught that France was the home of the greatest pastries and cakes. It was not until I worked in England, though, that I discovered the traditions behind the serving of particular cakes and pastries on particular occasions and learnt that the majority of delights served as part of afternoon tea originated in the United Kingdom. I loved this period of my life because it made me appreciate the simple things and some of the supposedly dull dishes in the pastry kitchen.

Fruit cake had never meant much to me — we only ate it at Christmas. However, with connoisseurs eating it daily for afternoon tea at the English hotel I worked in, our fruit cake was loved and was expected to be perfect. It was never served fresh from the oven, but was stored to mature and be served at the peak of its flavour. This recipe, however, makes a fruit cake that can be served straight away or stored and served later.

As traditional as scones with jam and clotted cream, or Swiss roll, a fruit cake is something that should be part of every High Tea.

Preheat the oven to 180°C (350°F). Grease a 23 x 10 x 10 cm (9 x 4 x 4 in) loaf pan lightly with butter and line it with baking paper (parchment).

Combine the flour, baking powder, cinnamon and cloves, and sift the mixture at least twice.

Cream the butter and sugar in a large bowl until light and creamy.

Add the marmalade and one of the eggs to the creamed butter and sugar, and stir until well combined. Add the remaining eggs, one at a time, combining well after each addition.

Combine all the dried fruit and dust it with a little of the flour mixture to prevent it sinking to the bottom of the cake.

Mix the fruit and chopped almonds with the remaining flour mixture, then add this to the creamed butter mixture. Stir until the mixture is combined, then spoon the cake mixture into the prepared pan.

Bake the cake for 2 hours, or until a skewer inserted into the centre comes out clean.

Let the cake cool in the pan for 20 minutes, then turn it out onto a wire rack. Let it cool for another hour before serving. The fruit cake is best cut into thin slices.

Jalousie

The first jalousie I tasted was this almond and raspberry recipe from England.

Almost any fruit combination goes well with the almond base.

Preheat oven to 180°C (350°F). Line a baking tray (sheet) with baking paper (parchment). Roll the pastry on a lightly floured bench surface until it is 47 x 25 cm (19 x 10 in). Cut the pastry in half lengthwise. Place one of the strips on the baking tray.

Leave the second strip of pastry on the bench surface. Use a small sharp knife to cut rows of 2 to 3 cm (1 in) slits into the pastry, down its length. Start 2 cm (¾ in) from one edge. Leave about 1 cm (½ in) between the slits (vertically), and about 1 cm (½ in) between the rows of slits (horizontally). Stagger the alternate rows of slits (making a pattern like brickwork). When cooked the pastry will have a lattice-style appearance. Chill the pastry pieces while you prepare the filling.

Filling

In a bowl, beat the butter and sugar until creamy, light and fluffy. Add the egg and beat for 3 minutes. Stir in the flour and almonds.

Apricot Glaze

Stir together the apricot jam and the water. In a saucepan, heat the mixture. Let it boil for 2 to 3 minutes, or until the apricot is the consistency of a glaze.

Brush half the egg along the edges of the pastry strip on the tray.

Spread the filling mixture evenly along the centre of the pastry. Press the raspberries into the almond mixture, then cover the jalousie with the second strip of pastry, stretching it lightly to open the lattice design slightly.

Brush the top of the pastry with the remainder of the egg.

Bake for 50 to 55 minutes, or until both base and top are cooked. While still hot, brush the top and sides with apricot glaze and sprinkle the sides with flaked almonds. Cool on the tray on a wire rack.

Serves 12

375 g (12 oz) prepared
puff pastry

Filling

155 g (5 oz) unsalted butter

⅔ cup (155 g/5 oz) sugar

1 egg

1¼ cups (155 g/5 oz)
plain (all-purpose) flour

1⅓ cups (155 g/5 oz)
ground (minced) almonds

125 g (4 oz)
fresh or frozen raspberries

1 egg, lightly beaten

½ cup (185 g/6 oz) apricot jam

3 tablespoons water

60 g (2 oz) flaked almonds,
roasted

Strawberry Delice

This sensational dessert is normally cut into thin fingers and served with fresh fruits, but it is also served as a light dessert for afternoon tea. It is light enough not to spoil your appetite, and is a dessert you will never forget.

Base

185 g (6 oz) unsalted butter

⅔ cup (155 g/5 oz) sugar

3 eggs

1 egg yolk

1½ cups (185 g/6 oz) ground almonds

2 tablespoons plain (all-purpose) flour, sifted

2 level teaspoons cornflour (cornstarch)

Filling

475 ml (15 fl oz) strawberry purée

250 ml (8 fl oz) sugar syrup (see page 113)

25 g (¾ oz) powdered gelatine

¼ cup (60 ml/2 fl oz) water

1½ cups (375 ml/12 fl oz) single (light) cream

Topping

1 cup (310 ml /10 fl oz) raspberry purée

10 g (⅓ oz) powdered gelatine

3 tablespoons water

Base

Preheat the oven to 180°C (350°F). Line a 30 x 30 cm (12 x 12 in) baking tray (sheet) with baking paper (parchment).

In a bowl (you can also use a small food processor), beat the butter and sugar until well creamed. Add the eggs and egg yolk and combine well. Finally, add the ground almonds, flour and cornflour, and mix until combined.

Spread the mixture onto the baking tray.

Bake for 12 to 15 minutes, or until lightly golden brown around the edges, but white and firm to the touch in the centre.

Cool on the tray. Cut a 23 cm (9 in) circle using the inside edge of a springform pan as a guide. Place the cut cake in the bottom of the springform pan.

Filling

Mix the gelatine and water in a small bowl. Stand the bowl in a pan of hot water until the gelatine dissolves.

Place the strawberry purée and the sugar syrup in a saucepan and bring to the boil.

Remove from the heat and add the gelatine mixture. Stir until the gelatine dissolves. Place the liquid in the refrigerator until it is cool to the touch.

Whisk the cream until it forms stiff peaks, then fold in the strawberry mixture.

Pour the mixture onto the baked cake disc. Place the dessert in the refrigerator for 1 to 2 hours, or until the fillling is firm to the touch.

Topping

Soak the gelatine in the water until it is dissolved.

In a small saucepan, heat the raspberry purée until it is simmering. Add the soaked gelatine and stir until it dissolves. Let the raspberry mixture cool. When it is cool to the touch, pour it quickly over the strawberry mousse. Refrigerate the dessert again, for 20 to 30 minutes, until the glaze has set.

Remove the springform ring and slide the delice off the springform base.

Serve the delice in wedges (or use a hot knife to cut it into squares) with fresh cream and sugar-dipped berries.

Serves 10 to 12

Strawberry Delice

Lemon Meringue Tart

Every tea trolley has at some stage included the famous Lemon Meringue Tart, made either as one large tart or as individual tartlets. This dessert combines the sharpness of lemons with the sweet, light and airy texture of meringue to make a tart like no other.

If you like to experiment, use oranges instead of lemons, or make your own chocolate filling — you will still have a meringue pie from heaven!

Pastry Case

2 cups (250 g /8 oz) plain (all-purpose) flour, sifted

½ cup (90 g/3 oz) icing (powdered) sugar

155 g (5 oz) unsalted butter, chopped into 1 cm (½ in) cubes

2 egg yolks

Filling

3 tablespoons cornflour (cornstarch)

2 tablespoons plain (all-purpose) flour

1¼ cups (310 ml/10 fl oz) water

zest and juice of 3 lemons

4 egg yolks

½ cup (125 g/4 oz) sugar

Meringue

3 egg whites

¼ cup (60 g/2 oz) sugar

Pastry Case

Preheat the oven to 190°C (375°F).

Place the flour and icing sugar in a bowl with the butter. Rub the butter into the dry ingredients until the mixture resembles coarse breadcrumbs.

Add the egg yolks and work the mixture to a dough. Wrap the dough in plastic wrap (cling film) and refrigerate it for 40 minutes.

On a lightly floured board, roll the pastry to a 2 to 3 mm (⅒ in) thickness, so it will easily fit into a 20 to 23 cm (8 to 9 in) pie plate or flan ring.

Line the pastry with greaseproof paper and weigh it down with baking weights or rice. Bake for 15 to 20 minutes, or until it is golden brown around the edges and baked through on the base.

Remove the pastry from the oven when it is cooked, but leave the oven turned on. Take out the paper and baking weights and let the base cool.

Filling

Blend the cornflour and plain flour with a little of the water to make a thin paste. Put the rest of the water on to boil with the lemon juice and zest. Pour the boiling mixture over the blended mixture, stirring well. Return the mixture to the saucepan and cook, still stirring, for 2 minutes.

Take the mixture off the heat and quickly stir in the egg yolks and sugar. Whisk until the sugar is dissolved, then pour the mixture into the precooked pastry base.

Meringue

In a clean bowl, whisk the egg whites until they form stiff peaks. Slowly add the sugar and keep whisking until a glossy meringue has formed.

Pile the meringue on top of the lemon mixture and place the tart in the oven for 10 to 12 minutes, to set the meringue and lightly brown the crust.

Serve warm or refrigerate for 1 hour and serve cold.

Serves 12 to 16

Meringue

Meringue is one of the most fascinating mixtures anyone can make. There are several types of meringue, from the simple (whisked egg whites and sugar) to the more advanced (egg whites and sugar syrup for an Italian meringue). Because they are so simple, everyone can soon be an expert.

This meringue recipe is simple, quick and can blend with almost any flavours. For success every time, make certain that all your equipment is free of oil and grease and is spotlessly clean before you start.

9 egg whites

2½ cups (625 g/20 oz) sugar

a little cornflour (cornstarch)

whipped cream and berries, to serve

Preheat the oven to 125°C (250°F).

Place the egg whites in a clean, grease-free mixing bowl. Whisk until the egg whites are fluffy and hold stiff peaks.

Slowly drizzle the sugar into the mixture, still whisking, and continue whisking until the sugar is dissolved. The finished mixture should be stiff and quite glossy.

Place the mixture in a piping bag (pastry) bag (see page 126) fitted with a 1 cm (½ in) plain nozzle.

Line baking trays with baking paper (parchment), then lightly dust the trays with cornflour.

Pipe a 7 cm (3 in) disc of the meringue mixture, then pipe one layer higher around the edges to make a basket. There should be enough mixture for 15 baskets.

Bake the meringues for 1 hour, then turn off the heat and let the meringues dry in the cooling oven.

Remove the meringues from the oven and from the trays.

To serve, fill the meringues with fresh berries and whipped cream.

Makes 15 meringue baskets

Rum Babas

The baba, cousin to the savarin, is a rich, sweet pastry which should be served warm with fresh whipped cream (and a fork!).

I can remember looking with astonishment at the vast selection of flavour combinations and shapes of babas in the windows of a pastry shop in Amsterdam. They were served with different, intensely flavoured syrups, so even though the base was exactly the same, the babas took on completely different characteristics. The fruits can also be changed, for variation.

⅔ cup (125 g/4 oz) sultanas (golden raisins)

¼ cup (60 ml/2 fl oz) rum

30 g (1 oz) fresh (compressed) yeast

½ cup (125 ml/4 fl oz) lukewarm milk

4 cups (500 g/1 lb) strong (bread) flour

¼ teaspoon salt

6 eggs, lightly beaten

250 g (8 oz) unsalted butter, cut into 2.5 cm (1 in) cubes

2 tablespoons sugar

Syrup

2 cups (500 ml/16 fl oz) water

1¼ cups (310 g/10 oz) sugar

1 cup (250 ml/8 fl oz) sauterne

2 cinnamon sticks

5 whole cloves

roughly chopped zest of 1 lemon

Soak the sultanas in the rum overnight.

Preheat the oven to 180°C (350°F). Lightly butter ten 250 ml (8 fl oz) dariole moulds.

Place the milk and yeast in a small bowl and mix to dissolve the yeast.

Place the flour, salt and eggs in a mixing bowl. Add the yeast liquid and mix well for about 5 minutes, until the mixture is very smooth and very elastic.

Sprinkle the butter and the sugar on top of the mixture and leave the bowl in a warm area for 20 to 25 minutes, until the dough has doubled in size.

Mix the dough again for 2 to 3 minutes, until the butter and sugar are well incorporated. Fold through the sultanas, then pipe or spoon the mixture evenly into the buttered moulds. Let the babas sit on a tray in a warm area for 30 to 35 minutes, or until double in size, then bake them for 15 to 18 minutes, or until they are golden brown.

Remove the babas from the dariole moulds and let them cool slightly. Soak them in the prepared syrup, then serve immediately.

Syrup

Place all the syrup ingredients in a large saucepan and bring to the boil.

Stir until the sugar is dissolved, then let the syrup simmer for 10 to 15 minutes.

Pour the syrup into a baking dish and let it cool slightly. Roll each baba in the syrup, and pour over more syrup if required.

Serve the babas on individual plates or in paper cake cases.

Serves 10

Rum Babas

Mocha Eclairs

Crisp, hollow choux pastry is delicious by itself, but with this coffee and mascarpone filling, it is even more irresistible.

Until I began working with an Austrian pastrychef who specialised in small pastries for buffets, I had never had great success working with choux pastry, so I had either avoided making it or waited for the pastrychef to go home and then tried. When things didn't quite go the way they should, I blamed the oven or the mixture.

Today, having found the secret of success, choux pastry is a favourite of mine: do not use sugar in the choux paste, and bake the éclairs for longer than usual. The éclairs will still brown, from the caramelisation of natural sugars in the flour, but they won't burn so easily, and the longer they cook the more they will dry out.

You should not have to cut the choux pastries in half or remove mixture from the centre to dry them out. With this recipe, when you take them out of the oven, all you need to do is cool them, fill them and serve them.

If you have failed before try them again — don't let them beat you!

Choux Pastry

1½ cups (375 ml/12 fl oz) water

155 g (5 oz) unsalted butter

1¼ cups (155 g/5 oz) plain (all-purpose) flour

5 eggs, lightly beaten

Filling

310 g (10 oz) mascarpone cheese

½ cup (125 ml/4 fl oz) single (light) cream

2 tablespoons sugar

1 tablespoon instant coffee granules

1½ tablespoons hot water

1 quantity of chocolate doughnut glaze (see page 87)

Preheat oven to 200°C (400°F) and line a baking tray (sheet) with baking paper (parchment).

Place the water and butter in a saucepan and bring to the boil over medium heat. Remove from heat and add all the flour at once, beating all the time. Cook until the mixture leaves the sides of the saucepan, stirring all the time. Remove from the heat and gradually add the eggs, beating until the mixture is smooth, soft and shiny. Using a piping (pastry) bag fitted with a star shaped nozzle, pipe lengths of the mixture (about 2 cm/¾ in high and 6 cm/2½ in long) onto the prepared tray. (You can also loop the pastry to give each piece a mounded effect.) Bake for 45 to 50 minutes, or until the éclairs are puffed, brown and crisp. (Do not open the oven for the first 20 minutes.)

Leave the éclairs on the tray, and let them cool on a wire rack.

Filling

Combine the mascarpone, cream and sugar and mix until smooth.

Dissolve the coffee granules in the hot water, then stir this into the mascarpone mixture. Chill until required.

When the éclairs are cool, dip their tops into the chocolate glaze mixture. Place them in the refrigerator to let the glaze set, then cut them in half and use the piping bag to fill them with the coffee filling.

Makes 12 to 14

Palmiers

Quick, simple and delicious, these puff pastry treats are as fascinating to make as they are to eat.

To serve as a sweet snack, make them small, or make them larger for a dessert, or as an accompaniment to a mousse or a cream-style dessert.

375 g (12 oz) prepared
puff pastry

⅔ cup (155 g/5 oz) sugar

1 egg, lightly whisked

Preheat the oven to 180°C (350°F). Line two baking trays (sheets) with baking paper (parchment).

On a lightly floured bench roll the puff pastry to a 2 to 3 mm (⅒ in) thickness and a 30 to 40 cm (12 to 16 in) width.

Brush the puff pastry with lightly beaten egg and sprinkle on about one-third of the sugar.

Fold the long edges of the pastry in so that they meet in the centre. Using a rolling pin, gently press the two layers together.

Brush again with lightly beaten egg and then sprinkle again with sugar.

Again bring the two long edges together in the middle, then roll the pastry again to flatten it.

Brush the pastry strip with the egg again and sprinkle with sugar, then bring one side to join the other.

With the pastry strip on its side, a little like a Swiss roll, and using a sharp knife, cut the pastry into 1 cm (¾ in) slices. Place these, cut side down, on a baking tray. Leave room (2 to 3 cm/1 in) between the palmiers so they can spread.

Bake for 10 to 12 minutes, then remove the tray and, using a palette knife, turn the palmiers over. Place the tray back in the oven for 5 minutes, or until the palmiers are golden brown.

Remove the palmiers from the oven and serve them warm with fresh cream and marinated berries, or let them cool and serve them as an accompaniment to chocolate mousse, or sweet cream desserts, or ice cream.

Makes 12 to 14

ACCOMPANIMENTS

A dessert should never be swamped with sauce, nor should the sauce ever overpower the flavour and taste of the dessert: it should merely complement the dessert by making it moist and tasty.

These recipes for some of the more popular sauces and other extras will add that special something to make your ice cream, sorbet, mousse, pudding or pastry a hit.

Marinated Berries

Place the Grand Marnier, sauterne, water, sugar and orange juice and zest in a saucepan and bring to the boil.

Simmer gently for 2–3 minutes.

Add the berries and cook for a further 1 minute, then remove from the heat and refrigerate the mixture until cold.

Serve small pots of the marinated berries as an accompaniment to almost any dessert.

3 tablespoons Grand Marnier

2 tablespoons sauterne

½ cup (125 ml/4 fl oz) water

¼ cup (60 g/2 oz) sugar

juice and zest of 1 orange

500 g (1 lb) mixed berries (strawberries, raspberries, blueberries, etc.)

Cherry Compote

Preheat the oven to 175°C (345°F).

Place all the ingredients in a large ovenproof dish. Cover the dish, then cook in the preheated oven for 45 minutes. Remove from the oven and stir every 10 minutes during the 45 minutes.

Remove and cool, then serve warm or cold with the dessert.

625 g (1¼ lbs) fresh cherries (stoned)

½ cup (125 ml/4 fl oz) red wine

2 tablespoons port

¼ cup (60 g/2 oz) sugar

juice and zest of 1 orange

½ teaspoon cinnamon

Sugar Syrup

Place the sugar and water in a saucepan and bring to the boil. Boil the mixture for 2 minutes, or until it is reduced by half. Let the mixture cool.

Makes 1 cup (250 ml/8 fl oz)

1 cup (250 g/8 oz) sugar

1 cup (250 ml/8 fl oz) water

Marinated Berries

Previous page (left to right): Chocolate Baskets, page 122, Shortbread Biscuits, page 122, Chocolate Sauce, page 114, Vanilla Anglaise, page 117, and Tuile Cups, page 120

Chocolate Sauce

1 cup (250 ml/8 fl oz) water

½ cup (125 g/4 oz) sugar

60 g (2 oz) dark (plain or semi-sweet) chocolate

75 ml (2½ fl oz) water, extra

50 g (1¾ oz) cocoa powder, sifted

1 tablespoon cornflour (cornstarch)

⅓ cup (90 g/3 oz) sugar, extra

Place the water, sugar and chocolate in a saucepan and bring to the boil, stirring continuously.

Meanwhile, in a bowl, mix the extra water with the cocoa, cornflour and sugar.

When the liquid boils, whisk it quickly into the cornflour mixture. Return the combined mixture to the saucepan and bring it to the boil again, still stirring.

Remove the sauce from the heat and serve hot or cold.

Makes 2 cups (500 ml/16 fl oz)

Coffee Sauce

4 tablespoons golden syrup (treacle)

4 tablespoons brown sugar

30 g (1 oz) unsalted butter

2 tablespoons hot water

1 tablespoon instant coffee granules

2 tablespoons arrowroot

2 cups (500 ml/16 fl oz) milk

Place the golden syrup, sugar and butter in a saucepan and bring to the boil, stirring occasionally to dissolve the sugar.

Simmer for several minutes, until the syrup looks golden around the edges of the saucepan. Then remove from the heat.

In a cup, stir the water and instant coffee into a paste.

In a bowl, combine the arrowroot, coffee mixture and milk, then slowly stir this into the syrup.

Return the pan to the heat and bring back to the boil, stirring. Simmer the sauce until it thickens, then strain and serve.

Makes 3 cups (250 ml/24 fl oz)

Caramel Sauce

1⅔ cups (310 g/10 oz) brown sugar

¼ cup (60 g/2 oz) sugar

60 g (2 oz) unsalted butter

1 cup (250 ml/8 fl oz) double (whipping) cream

Place all the ingredients in a saucepan and bring to the boil while stirring. Boil for 4 to 5 minutes, then remove from the heat and serve.

Makes 2 to 3 cups (500 to 750 ml/16 to 24 fl oz)

Treacle or Butterscotch Sauce

Place all the ingredients in a saucepan and bring slowly to the boil. Let the sauce simmer and reduce until it is the consistency of double (whipping) cream.

Makes 3 cups (750 ml/24 fl oz)

2 cups (500 m/16 fl oz) single (light) cream

2 tablespoons golden syrup (treacle)

1¼ cups (310 g/10 oz) demerara sugar

Lemon Sauce

Place the lemon juice and zest, water and sugar in a saucepan. Stir until the sugar dissolves.

Take 50 ml of the liquid and, in a separate bowl, mix it with the arrowroot, until you have a smooth paste.

Bring the liquid to the boil and, while boiling, quickly whisk in the arrowroot mixture.

Reboil for 1 to 2 minutes, then remove from the heat.

When the mixture is lukewarm, whisk through the egg yolk. Strain the sauce and let it cool slightly, then serve.

Makes 1 to 1½ cups (250–375 ml/8–12 fl oz)

juice and finely grated zest of 2 lemons

1 cup (250 ml/8 fl oz) water

30 g (1 oz) caster (superfine) sugar

1 tablespoon arrowroot

20 g (¾ oz) unsalted butter

1 egg yolk

Citrus Sauce

In a bowl, whisk the egg yolks and icing sugar until they are light, fluffy and creamy in colour. Whisk the orange and lemon juice and the cream into the egg yolk mixture.

Fold through the rum and serve the sauce immediately with your favourite pudding.

Makes 4 to 5 cups (1 litre/1¾ imp. pints)

5 egg yolks

¾ cup (125 g/4 oz) icing (powdered) sugar

1 cup (250 ml/8 fl oz) orange juice

juice of 1 lemon

2¼ cups (540 ml/18 fl oz) double (whipping) cream, lightly whipped

2 tablespoons rum

Vanilla Anglaise

1 cup (250 ml/8 fl oz)
single (light) cream

1 cup (250 ml/8 fl oz) milk

5 egg yolks

⅓ cup (60 g/2 oz) sugar

finely grated zest of 1 lemon

In a saucepan, heat the cream and milk until they boil.

In a bowl, lightly whisk the egg yolks, sugar and lemon zest.

Slowly whisk the boiled liquid into the egg yolk mixture. Pour the mixture back into the saucepan.

Stir the anglaise with a wooden spoon over low heat until it thickens and clings smoothly to the wooden spoon. Do not let the mixture simmer or boil.

Remove the anglaise from the heat and place the saucepan in iced water. Continue stirring until the mixture is cool. If necessary, strain the anglaise through muslin or a fine strainer.

Makes 3 cups (750 ml/24 fl oz)

Lemon Anglaise

1 cup (250 ml/8 fl oz)
single (light) cream

1 cup (250 ml/8 fl oz) milk

5 egg yolks

¼ cup (60 g/2 oz) sugar

finely grated zest of 2 lemons

Place the cream and milk in a saucepan and bring to the boil.

In a bowl, lightly whisk the egg yolks, sugar and lemon zest.

Remove the boiled liquid from the heat and slowly whisk it into the egg yolk mixture. Pour the mixture back into the saucepan.

Heat the anglaise over a low flame, stirring continuously (with a wooden spoon) until it thickens enough to cling smoothly to the spoon. Do not let the anglaise boil, or even simmer. Remove the saucepan from the heat and set it into iced water. Continue stirring until the anglaise is cool. If necessary, strain the anglaise through a muslin cloth or fine strainer.

Makes 3 cups (750 ml/24 fl oz)

Vanilla Anglaise with dots of Chocolate Sauce, page 114

Custard

2 cups (500 ml/16 fl oz) milk

¼ cup (60 g/2 oz) sugar

⅓ cup (90 ml/3 fl oz) milk, extra

2½ tablespoons cornflour
(cornstarch)

2 eggs

Place 2 cups (500 ml/16 fl oz) of milk and the sugar in a saucepan and bring to the boil.

Mix the extra milk with the cornflour. When a smooth paste has formed, add the eggs and whisk thoroughly.

Take the milk and sugar mixture off the heat and quickly whisk in the egg mixture.

Return the mixture to the heat and continue to stir until the mixture boils.

Serve immediately with a hot pudding.

Makes 3 cups (750 ml/24 fl oz)

Sweet White Sauce

60 g (2 oz) unsalted butter

½ cup (60 g/2 oz)
plain (all-purpose) flour

6 teaspoons sugar

1¼ cups (310 ml/10 fl oz) milk

zest of 1 lemon

Melt the butter. Add the flour and sugar and mix (away from the heat) to form a roux. Return the mixture to the heat for 1 to 2 minutes, stirring constantly to make sure it does not brown.

Slowly add the milk, stirring continuously, then bring to the boil. Remove from the heat, add the lemon zest, and serve immediately with puddings.

Makes 2 cups (500 ml/16 fl oz)

Variations

Orange: Substitute orange zest for the lemon zest.
Cinnamon: Add or substitute 1 teaspoon of ground cinnamon for the lemon zest.
Honey: Substitute honey or golden syrup (treacle) for the sugar.

Génoise Sponge

Preheat the oven to 180°C (350°F).

Sift the flour three times.

Grease a 23 cm (9 in) springform cake tin lightly with butter, then dust the tin with a little flour. Shake the tin to remove any excess flour.

Place the eggs, sugar and vanilla essence in the mixing bowl of an electric mixer and beat on the highest setting for 8 to 10 minutes, or until the mixture is thick, pale and fluffy.

Lightly sprinkle the flour over the mixture and very gently fold it through by hand. Pour the mixture into the prepared cake tin and bake for 30–35 minutes, or until the sponge has shrunk slightly away from the sides of the tin and the top springs back when lightly touched. Cool the sponge in the pan for 5 minutes, then turn it onto a wire rack to cool.

1¼ cups (155 g/5 oz) plain (all-purpose) flour

6 eggs

⅔ cup (155 g/5 oz) sugar

1 teaspoon vanilla essence

Langue de Chat Biscuits

Among the more traditional accompaniments to iced desserts, these long cat's tongue-shaped biscuits are crisp additions to any ice cream plate. These are also often used as spoons.

Preheat the oven to 180°C (350°F) and line two baking trays (sheets) with baking (parchment) paper.

In a bowl, cream the softened butter and icing sugar until light and fluffy and almost white.

In another bowl, whisk the egg whites with the sugar until they form stiff peaks. Fold the egg whites into the butter mixture, then add the sifted flour. Fold all together carefully.

Place the mixture in a piping (pastry) bag fitted with a 1 cm (½ inch) round nozzle, and pipe 7 cm (3 inch) lengths onto the baking trays. Allow plenty of room for spreading.

Bake for 10 to 12 minutes. Let the biscuits cool on the trays before removing and serving them.

These biscuits will keep in an airtight container for 2 to 3 days.

Makes 36

¾ cup (185 g/6 oz) unsalted butter, softened

1¼ cups (225 g/7 oz) icing (powdered) sugar, sifted

4 egg whites

¼ cup (60 g/2 oz) sugar

1¼ cups (155 g/5 oz) plain (all-purpose) flour, sifted

icing sugar, for dusting

Tuiles and Tuile Cups

¾ cup (155 g/5 oz)
icing (powdered) sugar

1 cup (125 g/4 oz)
plain (all-purpose) flour

3 egg whites

⅓ cup (90 g/3 oz)
unsalted butter, melted

*These biscuits often take the place of the spoon, being used to scoop up the ice cream.
Alternatively, simply mould the biscuit over a bowl, cup or glass while it is still
warm and pliable. The biscuit will take on the shape of a basket,
thus creating a serving dish.*

Preheat the oven to 180°C (350°F) and line a baking tray (sheet) with baking paper (parchment).

In a bowl, sift together the icing sugar and the flour.

Add the egg whites and combine, until the mixture forms a stiff paste. Add the melted butter and combine well. Let the mixture rest for 5 minutes.

Spread a dessertspoonful of the mixture at a time onto the baking tray, in thin, even discs.

Bake for 5 to 8 minutes, or until just turning golden brown.

Remove the biscuits from the tray immediately, and drape them over bowls, cups or glasses, if baskets are required, or over a rolling pin if the traditional shape is required.

You can store finished biscuits and baskets in an airtight container for 1 to 2 days, but they are best made when required, and eaten fresh.

The mixture will store in the refrigerator for 1 to 2 weeks.

Makes 18 to 24

Chocolate Tuiles

6 egg whites

1 cup (185 g/6 oz) icing
(powdered) sugar, sifted

½ cup (60 g/2 oz) plain
(all-purpose) flour, sifted

1 tablespoon cocoa powder, sifted

75 g (2½ oz) unsalted butter,
melted

Preheat the oven to 180 C (350 F) and lightly grease a baking tray (sheet).

Mix the egg whites with the sifted icing sugar until incorporated. Add the flour and cocoa and lightly whisk, until a smooth batter is formed. Let the batter rest for 15 minutes. Stir in the melted butter and mix well. Place tablespoons of the batter on the baking tray and spread them into 5 to 8 cm (2 to 3 in) circles.

Bake for 10 minutes. Remove the tuiles from the baking tray by sliding a flat knife underneath each one.

Press each tuile immediately around a rolling pin or another cylindrical object so that it hardens into a semi-circular shape. If the tuiles become cold and firm before you have finished shaping them, reheat them on the baking tray in the oven to 1 to 2 minutes, or until they become soft and malleable.

Makes 18 to 24 tuiles

From bottom right, moving anti-clockwise: Tuiles, Shortbread Biscuits, page 122 and Langue de Chat Biscuits, page 119

Shortbread Biscuits

Pipe these in small rounds or in long fingers to serve with the mousse or dessert of your choice.

280 g (9 oz) unsalted butter

½ cup (90 g/3 oz) caster (superfine) sugar, plus extra, for dusting

280 g (9 oz) plain (all-purpose) flour

90 g (3 oz) cornflour (cornstarch)

Preheat the oven to 180°C (350°F). Line a baking tray (sheet) with baking paper (parchment).

In a bowl, cream the butter and the sugar until light and fluffy and almost white.

In another bowl, sift together the flour and the cornflour. Add this to the butter and sugar mixture and mix well. Scrape down the sides of the bowl so that all the butter and sugar is mixed into the flour.

Place the mixture in a piping (pastry) bag fitted with a 1 cm (½ in) star nozzle (piping tube). Pipe small rosettes onto the baking tray.

Bake for 8 to 10 minutes, or until the biscuits are just turning golden brown around the edges.

Sprinkle the biscuits with caster sugar immediately, then let them cool. Store in an airtight container.

Makes 24

Chocolate Baskets

A quick, simple, and tasty way of serving ice cream is to make a basket of chocolate and serve it filled with your favourite ice creams.

310 g (10 oz) dark (plain or semi-sweet) chocolate, melted

Use about 2 tablespoons of chocolate for each basket. Spread the chocolate in a circular shape over a piece of plastic (cut from a rubbish bin liner or freezer bag). Drape the disc of chocolate over a cup or mould. When the chocolate has set, carefully peel off the plastic, and the basket is ready to be used.

Makes about 6 baskets

Chocolate Curls

Pour melted dark chocolate onto a marble slab or a stainless steel bench (counter) top and use a palette knife to spread thinly. As the chocolate begins to set, hold a large knife at a 45 angle to the bench or surface and pull gently through the chocolate. It is essential to work quickly or the chocolate will harden and splinter. This will make enough curls to cover a 23 cm (9 in) cake.

500 g (16 oz) dark (plain or semi-sweet) chocolate

Roasted Flaked Almonds

Preheat the oven to 180 C (350 F).

Spread the almonds thinly on a baking tray (sheet). Bake for 4 minutes. Remove the tray and turn the almonds, using a fork. Return the tray to the oven and bake for a further 4 minutes. Remove the tray again and turn the almonds again. Continue this process until the almonds are golden brown. Let the almonds cool on the tray.

2½ cups (250 ml/8 oz) flaked almonds

White Butter Icing

Place the butter, icing sugar and glucose in a bowl and blend together slowly. When these ingredients are thoroughly mixed, slowly add the water and vanilla, little by little, mixing well after each addition. When all th water and vanilla have been added, beat the icing for 15 minutes at top speed, or until the icing is white, light and fluffy.

Keep the mixture well covered at all times, either with a damp cloth or by satoring it in an airtight container.

Makes enough to cover a 23 cm (9 in) cake

60 g (2 oz) unsalted butter

3 cups (540 g/18 oz) icing (powdered) sugar, sifted

1½ tablespoons liquid glucose (corn syrup)

¼ cup (60 ml/2 fl oz) water

1 teaspoon vanilla essence

Candied or Mixed Peel

2 oranges

2 lemons

1 cup (250 g/8 oz) sugar

155 ml (5 fl oz) water

2 tablespoons liquid glucose
(corn syrup)

Make sure that the oranges and lemons have clean skins. Using a sharp knife, carefully remove the skin. Try not to take too much of the white pith with it. When all the rind has been removed from the fruit, cut away any excess pith from the rind. Cut each of the strips of rind as thin as possible (1 to 2 mm/1/12 in).

Put the sugar, water and glucose into a saucepan and bring to the boil. Add the rind of the fruit and boil for a further 20 minutes. As the mixture boils, wash down the sides of the saucepan with a pastry brush dipped in warm water. Place the peel on a wire cooling rack and allow to drain and dry overnight. Once dried, cut the peel into small pieces and use it in cakes, puddings, dipped in chocolate or eaten by itself.

Makes 1 cup of peel

Rum Babas, page 106

HINTS

Hints

Ingredients

All ingredients should be at room temperature when used unless the recipe advises otherwise. Make sure that all your utensils are clean, dry and grease free before cooking. Water or grease on utensils can adversely affect recipes, especially when using egg whites, which will not reach maximum aeration if mixed with even small amounts of grease and water.

Egg weights

All eggs used in these recipes should be 60 g (2 oz).

Making a Paper Piping (Pastry) Bag

Begin making your piping bag with a triangular piece of baking paper (parchment). Take the top corner of the paper and roll it along the longest edge. Pinch the point of the roll with one hand and continue rolling the paper with the other. When all the paper has been rolled, tuck the remaining flap inside the cone. Cut a small point from the end of the bag. If a larger opening is required, cut small pieces from the tip until you have the size you need; if too large a tip is cut, the filling may run out too easily. For the best results, fill the bag only half full with mixture.

Yeast

Fresh compressed yeast is preferable to dried yeast in all recipes that use yeast. However, if you cannot get fresh yeast, use dried yeast. If you are using dried yeast, add the flour and dry ingredients, then add liquid.

15 g ($\frac{1}{2}$ oz) dried yeast equals 30 g (1 oz) fresh yeast (Follow the packet instructions if they differ from this.)

Index